EDINBURGH PUBLIC LIBRARIES

FINE ART LIBRARY
GEORGE FOURTH BRIDGE

HOME READING SECTION

Architect and Community

Contemporary Issues Series

GEOFFREY SPYER

Architect and Community

ENVIRONMENTAL DESIGN IN AN URBAN SOCIETY

PETER OWEN · LONDON

ISBN 0 7206 0290 4

PETER OWEN LIMITED
12 Kendrick Mews Kendrick Place London SW7

First British Commonwealth edition 1971
© Geoffrey Spyer 1971

Printed in Great Britain by
Bristol Typesetting Co Ltd
Barton Manor St Philips Bristol

Contents

Illustrations

facing page 128

Lillington Street, Pimlico

Churchill Gardens, Pimlico

facing page 129

Waterford Road and Fulham Road, London

The illustrations in this volume are reproduced by kind permission of the following:

The Architectural Press Ltd for the photographs of Walter Gropius (photo Sam Lambert); Frank Lloyd Wright (photo Sam Lambert); Livingston, Scotland (photo Wm J. Toomey); CLASP school, Milan Trienale (photo K. G. Browne); CLASP system, York University (photo de Burgh Galwey); Essex University (photo Wm J. Toomey); Roehampton, Surrey (photo Wm J. Toomey); Park Hill, Sheffield (photo Wm J. Toomey); Lillington Street, Pimlico (photo de Burgh Galwey); Churchill Gardens, Pimlico (photo Henk Snook Photography & Associates).

The Greater London Council Print Collection for the pictures of I. K. Brunel and William Morris.

Her Majesty's Stationery Office for the photograph of Habitat, Montreal (model), and for the four photographs of industrialized housing in Eastern Europe, all of which are Crown copyright.

The Irish Tourist Office for the photograph of Georgian houses in Merrion Square, Dublin (Bord Failte photo, reproduction rights reserved).

The Royal Institute of British Architects, Sir Banister Fletcher Library, for the photographs of the drawings by Joseph Paxton and Mies van der Rohe, and for the photograph (portrait) of Mies van der Rohe.

Acknowledgments

The idea of writing about the background to the architect's work in the community was suggested to Norman Sheppard and me by Mr W. Millington Synge in 1967. Norman Sheppard and I had originally planned to write this book jointly. Subsequently Norman Sheppard collaborated in the drafting of several chapters, and he has contributed material and comment throughout to such an extent that the book would probably not have been completed without his help. While I cannot overestimate his contribution, I must absolve him from responsibility for any errors or omissions.

I must thank my friend Mr W. J. Fishman for his encouragement in the early days and for enabling me to use the first chapters as the basis for various lectures to Workers' Educational Association groups in North London. I am also grateful to Mr Jeremy Eldridge for allowing me to expand these lectures into a course for Interior Design students at Hornsey College of Art. Miss Julie Ward contributed patient research into the subject of housing and Mr Richard Jones undertook the selection and collection of many of the illustrations.

Numerous friends and colleagues have knowingly or unknowingly supplied ideas and encouragement, but despite their universal concern with the problems of the environment, it would be unfair to suggest that they all share my views on causes and solutions.

G. S.

Introduction

Today we are at a particularly crucial phase of a major revolution in human society. At this present stage of the Industrial Revolution industrialization is reaching all parts of the world and human society is becoming urbanized on an international rather than on a national scale. We are only just beginning to realize the extent of the problems inherent in a largely man-made environment. Our thinking hitherto has been within very narrow limits. But as we step into space and, for the first time in history, look at the earth from outside, we are becoming aware of the need to examine urgently the environment we are creating as an overall problem which affects everyone and everything on this planet.

This is the last sphere of interest to which the tools and techniques that have been developed for modern science and industry are being applied. Since the dawn of industrialization, the needs of man have always tended to take second place to those of the machine: the environment has been almost completely subject to the direct and indirect demands of the machines and processes of industry and of its products. Science and technology, developed for and by the means of production, have never been directed seriously at those physical elements of the environment which were not immediately and materially productive.

Most of what we have built in the past 150 years has been haphazard and unplanned. Its ultimate effect has often been antisocial and inhuman. We have been consistently niggardly in our expenditure on buildings except for 'prestige' purposes. We have been blind to the fact that, as the environment becomes more man-made, we must think harder and spend more money if we are to satisfy the needs of a healthy society. Even today, few will argue over the spending of vast sums of money for a building to house a computer or a space rocket, but governments and individuals will go to endless lengths to reduce the costs of housing.

It has already been reported in Britain that the cost of buying and running a car is often as much as that of buying and maintaining a house. Clearly there is an imbalance somewhere, and from what one may learn of the past, it is evident that we are still spending far too little on housing. It is equally clear, and stated so often publicly as to need little emphasis here, that the root of many of the social problems in industrial societies lies in poor housing conditions. A reconsideration of the economic structure of society in relation to social priorities is therefore long overdue.

Meanwhile we have to ask what sort of environment we should be creating for an urbanized society. Many suggestions and ideas have been put forward and many studies and experiments are being carried out. I shall therefore examine briefly the history of urbanization and architecture over the past 150 years to see how the present situation has come about. I shall then examine critically some of the ideas at present being promoted and studied to see which of them may produce satisfactory solutions. In doing so I shall try to take into account all the factors which affect social development. As an architect, I am not of course fully enough equipped to consider in great detail such fields as sociology, economics, philosophy and physical science. The development of a satisfactory environment is not the sole responsibility of the architect. The prerequisite for comprehensive planning is to achieve a consensus of all the relevant disciplines. To reach such a consensus is likely to be the greatest problem. In the first place everyone concerned with the problem should understand its nature. One of my aims is to provoke others, expert in fields other than architecture, to consider the issues and some of the solutions I shall prescribe.

I am much concerned that future ideas of planning and building should take into account from the start the fact of change. Society is never at a standstill. Rigid planning theories will never produce satisfactory solutions. One of the obstacles in the way of meeting the requirements of a changing society is our tendency to create institutions, organizations, rules and regulations which, by their nature, resist change. An inordinate amount of time and energy has to be spent on circumventing these institutions in one way or another, in order to build anything worth while. In order to plan for a changing society, the dynamic thought and action which are necessary must be anti-institutional, in fact anti-Establishment, unless we can create institutions which are themselves dynamic. I shall, in the course of my study, question the role and even the existence of the various institutions which regulate the development of our environment.

My questioning the institutions and the economic structure of society suggests that I may be subversive in outlook, an attitude for which I make no apology. Many of the problems facing us in creating a human environment have to do with attitudes, assumptions and institutions and are not phenomena which happened in a process of natural evolution. It follows that we may well be able to solve the problems by evolving new attitudes and by thinking afresh about many of the assumptions on which our present society is based.

I lay no claim to be setting down any startling new ideas. Numerous volumes on the subject of cities, urbanization, industrialization, housing and planning have already been written, particularly over the last decade. My summary of the situation and how it has arisen, written from the point of view of someone actively engaged in the design and building of elements of the environment, has been undertaken as much for my own benefit as for my readers. With other architects, I need to clarify and understand the situation in which we are working and the implications of what we are doing. Other architects and specialists have or will doubtless undertake their own studies and researches from similar and wider sources and probably in greater depth than I have. But I hope this book will be of interest and of practical use to those who are not immediately concerned with the day-to-day problems of building. Inevitably we are all involved with our environment. The environment, the world about us, belongs to us all, not just to the planners and architects. The greater the degree of involvement of intelligent men generally, the greater the chance of avoiding disasters and of hope for the future.

Chapter 1

The Legacy of the Victorians

The nineteenth century witnessed the transformation of society in the Western world from agrarian to industrial, from rural to urban. The urbanization of Western society is now virtually complete and we are witnessing the same transformation in many other areas of the world. Within the foreseeable future, world society will be predominantly urban.

The process of urbanization in many parts of Western Europe and the United States has been largely unplanned, almost accidental, and the results have been chaotic, not to say disastrous. One writer claims that 'the main contribution of the Victorian age to architecture is the slum',[1] while another writes : '. . . never before in recorded history had such vast masses of people lived in such a savagely deteriorated environment, ugly in form, debased in content . . . never before had human blight so universally been accepted as normal : normal and inevitable'.[2]

How was it that the process of urbanization produced such a situation? To what extent were the results of urbanization due to the very nature of industrialization or to neglect, selfishness or stupidity? To what extent has urbanization in the nineteenth century left its mark on our own times? These are some of the questions I shall try to examine in the following pages. The history of city development from earliest times is the history of communication between men. Cities have always been meeting-places for men at road junctions, bridges, fords, passes, harbours and so on. As societies developed and became more stable, cities became

[1] Robert Furneaux Jordan, *Victorian Architecture* (Harmondsworth, Middx : Penguin Books, 1966).
[2] Lewis Mumford, *The City in History* (London : Secker & Warburg, 1961).

more important as centres of communication for trade, barter, the exchange of ideas, seats of government and administration.

The industrialization of society has depended on the development of improved means of transport and communication. It also produced an accelerated growth of population. These two factors are at the root of the pattern of expansion of our cities in the nineteenth century and their further development in this century into vast conurbations and urban regions. They are fundamental to the problems of urbanization.

The canals and turnpikes of eighteenth-century Britain were inadequate to cope with the demands of expanding industry. A means of transporting cheaply and speedily large volumes of fuel, raw materials and finished products was required to enable expansion to take place. Roads had to await the coming of oil, electricity and the invention of the internal combustion engine before they could make a significant contribution. Steam was the basic power source of the nineteenth century and the railway the new basic means of transport. Asa Briggs has written : 'The railway linked the new cities together and made their growth possible : like the cities themselves it was a symbol of improvement. . . . The first railways encouraged the concentration of urban population . . . the automobile, by contrast, scattered the cities pushing them farther and farther away from their mid-Victorian centres to new suburbs.'[3]

If steam was the source of power, iron was the raw material of the nineteenth century. Only with the technological development of iron, and later of steel, was it possible to make the railways, machines, bridges and buildings which were the tools of industry. This development had an enormous effect on architecture. In fact it has completely revolutionized building over the last hundred years and made possible a whole new range of architectural forms and concepts. It was during this period that what we call Modern Architecture was born.

The birth-place of modern architecture was in the great railway sheds of iron and glass that were built in the 1830s and later —St Pancras, Euston, Paddington, Kings Cross—and in the multi-storey mills with their cast-iron structures and massive classical

[3] Asa Briggs, *Victorian Cities* (London: Odhams Press, 1963).

brick exteriors, in the great railway viaducts and bridges. The high point of development of iron and glass structures was undoubtedly Joseph Paxton's Crystal Palace, erected for the Great Exhibition of 1851 in Hyde Park. To the modern architect this is a symbol of the greatest achievement of nineteenth-century architecture in the same way that the Parthenon symbolizes Ancient Greece and Chartres Cathedral medieval Western Europe. Significantly the Crystal Palace was also the first completely prefabricated building.

This new 'iron age' of architecture saw the re-emergence of the structure of a building as the basis of its form, in contrast to the stylistic concepts of form which had predominated since the Renaissance. Not since the great medieval cathedrals had buildings given such direct and powerful expression to their structure to an extent where the structure *was* the building : not since those same great cathedrals had any architect achieved such loftiness and lightness. In fact this new architecture of the nineteenth century was not the work of architects in the professional sense but of engineers. There developed a great gulf between engineer and architect, from which we are still suffering today and which has had a disruptive effect on building. Gradually the gulf is being bridged, but the process is a painful one, particularly for the architect.

In the nineteenth century architects, concerned as they were with church design, public buildings and the houses of the growing middle class, clashed and struggled among themselves over the virtues of neo-classical and neo-Gothic styles. In the process they evolved a particularly vigorous and even aggressive range of forms and details which exactly matched the attitudes and taste of their clients and patrons, the new businessmen and entrepreneurs. Until recently there was a considerable reaction against the 'vulgar', typically Victorian style. Indeed the later Victorians led by William Morris reacted against it themselves. Today, further removed in history from the period, we can appreciate some of the qualities which were obscured in the earlier reaction against Victoriana.

During the same period engineers developed buildings with the new materials, largely independent of the stylistic battles raging in architectural spheres. When they did clothe their iron structures, they did so usually in classical Georgian style. This highlights the social gap between engineer and architect. Engineers tended to come from industrial areas and served as apprentices in engineering works. The style they employed for their buildings was that of the older eighteenth-century mills and towns in which they had grown up. The architects, on the other hand, were very much of the middle classes, sharing their education and their participation in the cultural changes that were taking place. They naturally became deeply involved in the Romantic movement, and in many ways from this point stemmed the idea of the architect as the unpractical dreamer and aesthete and the engineer as the practical man.

Meanwhile both architect and engineer were caught up in the great turmoil of urbanization, both working directly or indirectly for those who were leading industrial development and the administration of industrial cities. But neither concerned himself with the great mass of building that took place to house the expanding population. The engineer was concerned primarily with the tools of the industrial age. The architect's social responsibility was limited to the class to which he belonged and from which he drew his clients. It was only after a section of the middle class began to develop a conscience about the effects of its growing activities, in other words with the emergence of the social reformers of the second half of the century, that the prevalent form, content and planning of housing were called into question. Hitherto, these aspects had been the responsibility of the speculative builder rather than a subject for professional consideration.

Local authorities did not, however, accept any appreciable level of responsibility for housing until after the First World War; and only after the Second World War did the architectural profession become deeply involved in housing programmes in the public and private sectors. Yet it was the houses which were the slums or which became the slums. It was and still is in housing that the worst effects of industrialization and urbanization are felt, and this holds as true for the so-called developing countries today as it did for nineteenth-century Britain. Indeed it still holds true for the developed countries, so much so that many people seem to have the idea that bad housing is a natural phenomenon, and that living under poor housing conditions is a normal and acceptable way of life.

It may seem strange that in nineteenth-century Britain, side by side with the most appalling urban housing conditions, there developed in the expanding industrial cities a great sense of civic pride among the leaders of the community. The political movement which led to the Reform Bill of 1832 was closely associated with the movement that led to the Municipal Reform Act of 1835. The effect of this Act was the establishment of new cities of the industrial age, like Birmingham and Manchester, and the transference of power in older established cities, like Leicester, to the new men of the age—the industrialists rather than the landowners. The civic pride of these men was expressed in strange ways. The first priority was usually a strong police force; the second was to spend as little as possible on general public works; third was the building of a town hall. Joseph Strutt, Mayor of the newly elected Town Council of Derby in 1835, stated at his first public dinner that the Council's duties, in order of precedence, were to establish an efficient police force and to be as economical as possible.

Two factions dominated the political life of the new councils, and these often cut across the party divisions. One faction was for, the other against, improvements of a general nature. There was violent conflict on basic issues, the provision of water supplies and sanitation, even though Parliament had established machinery at local level for considering and recommending improvements through the Improvement Commissioners. Eventually epidemic disease, the direct result of inadequate water supplies and bad or non-existent sanitation, reached such proportions that it menaced the comfortable lives of the middle class. Cholera was an ever-present danger in the middle of the century and clearly persisted for longer periods in the overcrowded cities than in the villages. The connection between overcrowding and disease was inescapable. In Leeds in 1840 the average life expectancy of an upper-class male was forty-four years; of a middle-class male twenty-seven years; and of a working-class male nineteen years.[4]

Consequently, ideas for reform were seen strictly in terms of hygiene. From the 1830s onwards improvements were basically cleansing operations. Agitation during the 1840s led to the regulation

[4] For a description of working-class living standards and their decline between 1790 and 1840 see E. P. Thompson, *The Making of the English Working Class* (London: Gollancz, 1965).

of building under the Public Health Acts which set improved standards of hygiene and authorized the condemning of unfit property—slum clearance. The latter only aggravated the problems of overcrowding, since no provision was made for rehousing people thus displaced. There was mounting pressure for space in the centres of the cities partly to meet commercial demands and partly those of the railways for the construction of terminuses with yards and sidings. Considerable advantage was taken of official slum clearance to make land available for commercial development, which in turn encouraged the building of residential suburbs. The only problem was that the slum-dwellers could not afford the rents in the new suburbs so that other central areas became overcrowded and rents rose steadily.

The part played by railway development in this process was significant, since, as I have already suggested, transport has always been a crucial factor in urbanization. In London, for example, the land needs of the railways displaced many working men in the areas of the northern terminuses—St Pancras was built on the site of a working-class housing area (Somerstown), Kings Cross on the site of a fever hospital. Land farther in towards the centre was owned by the great landowners of pre-industrial times and was too expensive for the railways. In order to compensate for the displacement of so many working-class houses an Act of Parliament was passed (Cheap Trains Act 1883), by which the railway companies were obliged to allow cheap fares for working men, enabling them to live farther from their place of work and to commute. There was a rapid spread of suburban railways in North and East London, accompanied by the development of vast areas of housing beyond the earlier limits. The situation was neatly and significantly summed up by the General Manager of the Great Eastern Railway Company in evidence before the Royal Commission in 1885 :

Wherever you locate the workmen in large numbers you utterly destroy that neighbourhood for ordinary passenger traffic. Take, for instance, the neighbourhood of Stamford Hill, Tottenham and Edmonton. That used to be a very nice district indeed, occupied by good families, with houses of from £150 to £250 a year, with coach-houses and stables and gardens and a few acres of land. But very soon after this obligation was put upon the Great Eastern Company and accepted by the Great Eastern Company of issuing workmen's tickets, speculative builders went down into the neighbourhood, and, as a consequence, each good house was one after another pulled down, and the district is given up entirely, I may say, now to the working man.

The Great Eastern Company ran more workmen's trains than any other company and was the first to foresee the profits that could be made out of commuter services. Perhaps for this reason North-East London developed more rapidly than any other part as a working-class area.

Poor housing was one of the basic costs of nineteenth-century economic expansion and one of the worst legacies of the Victorians, not only in Britain but in many cities of the United States and Western Europe. H.J. Dyos has written: 'Houses built for one class went through the hands of other classes with diminishing suitability. The end product was the slum.'

One of the obstacles to effective solutions was the nineteenth-century idea of charitable rather than State help, an idea which is far from dead today. Coupled with this were notions of the deserving and the undeserving poor; those deserving of charity and those not deserving. In 1883 a pamphlet by an obscure clergyman, Andrew Mearns, *Bitter Outcry of Outcast London*, produced a violent public reaction which led to a Royal Commission on the Housing of the Working Classes (report 1885). It was to this Commission that the General Manager of the Great Eastern Railway Company gave evidence. But the Royal Commission failed to find an answer to the financial difficulties induced by slum clearance and redevelopment by local authorities largely because the idea of State aid could not be accepted even if it was conceivable. Ideas for reform were essentially paternalistic. It was after all from this period of the 1880s that the 'coal in the bath' idea stemmed. It was also in this period that the charitable trusts made attempts at solving the problem. The Housing Act of 1890, resulting from the Royal Commission, achieved little. Up to 1909 'back-to-back' housing was still permissible. Overcrowding of houses was not a punishable offence until 1935. The idea of the Local Authority becoming a landlord of low-cost houses was slow to be accepted. Even so, by 1910 7 per cent of working-class families in London were tenants of the London County Council.

The charitable trusts became involved in a programme of constructing 'improved dwellings'. Flats were a well-known form of accommodation in Scotland and on the Continent, but were unfamiliar in England, where, because of the housing shortage, it was usual for more than one working-class family to occupy a house. But houses were still built according to the traditional form for a single-family dwelling, with all the facilities on the ground floor or in the basement. The blocks of 'model dwellings for artisans' were the first to provide self-contained accommodation on one floor. Several stages of development occurred before the block of flats emerged as a distinct type of building. The first model dwellings, two-storey terraces built by the Society for Improving the Conditions of the Labouring Classes, were shown in miniature at the Great Exhibition of 1851. By the 1880s blocks of five and six storeys were an established building form, and attracted much criticism for their barrack- or prison-like appearance. The charities which provided model dwellings on a large scale tended to use the same design for a whole series of blocks and such repetition was disliked and criticized. The report of the Royal Commission of 1885 claimed that the working classes themselves disliked the excessive plainness of the buildings.

Although architects were frequently used by the charities to design their model dwellings in the latter part of the century, they appeared to be unable to handle successfully the problem of design. As I have said, the profession as a whole was concerned with rather more flamboyant and luxurious problems and seemed unable to raise much enthusiasm about the design of buildings where strict economy was the rule. The *Times*, commenting upon the results of a competition held by the Improved Industrial Dwellings Company for one of its buildings, remarked that 'the Company cannot find an architect who will be sufficiently modest in his aims to design the sort of building they require . . . to be economic is too hard, too demeaning for the profession'. The *Builder* said this remark was undeserved but elsewhere spoke of 'continental architects who had solved the problem of housing numerous families economically under one roof . . . ordinary Londoners have no idea how to plan a block'.

One of the other problems arising out of the work of the charities was that densities of housing were higher in the new developments than in the slums they had replaced. The following figures, giving average densities in two areas of London in 1874, are typical:

Westminster: 237 persons per acre
Spitalfields: 304 persons per acre

Comparable densities in some building estates of charitable trusts were:

Metropolitan Housing Association: 1,000 to 1,600 persons per acre
Peabody Estates: 459 to 1,000 persons per acre

These fantastically high densities (the normal maximum permitted density in limited parts of central London today is 200 persons per acre and is generally about 125 persons per acre) were achieved at the expense of adequate daylight and open space around the buildings. It is interesting that contemporary criticism was centred on the risk of the spread of infectious disease as the result of so many families living in close proximity.

There were, of course, slums during the nineteenth century in the United States. Their development was closely related to successive waves of immigration. Recent arrivals from overseas were generally forced to live in the poorest neighbourhoods. Tenement houses were started in the 1830s as a means of providing high-density housing. According to Mumford, the first tenement building in New York was built in 1835. The tenement house introduced the most notorious type of slum in the United States, in contrast to the back-to-back house slum in England. The worst and most common type of tenement was the 'railroad' type, in which 75 per cent of the rooms had no natural daylight or ventilation except by doors opening into rooms in the front or back of the building. This form of tenement became common in the second half of the century.

Particularly bad conditions existed in New York for three

reasons : (1) the geographical limitations imposed by the confines of the island of Manhattan, (2) the need of immigrants, who were usually very poor, to live close to their place of work, and (3) the form of subdivision of the city into 25 ft x 100 ft lots, imposed by the Commissioners' Plan of 1811. It was virtually impossible to construct high-rise buildings upon these plots without sacrificing light and air.

The first recorded reference to bad housing was made in a report by a New York City health inspector in 1834. He drew attention to the relationship between bad housing conditions, the spread of epidemics and high death-rate. His report was followed by more extensive and more emphatic ones by his successors. As a result the Association for Improving the Conditions of the Poor was founded. The Association conducted a survey which, in 1847, reported that the tenements of the poor were defective in size, arrangement, water supply, warmth and ventilation, and that rents were disproportionately high. In 1857 the State Legislature undertook an investigation, but it took ten years before any law was enacted. In 1867 it became illegal in New York to build a tenement house covering 100 per cent of its plot; a 10 ft yard had to be left at the rear of the building for light and air; a wholly subterranean room could no longer be rented for human habitation, the ceiling must be at least one foot above kerb level; city water must be available somewhere on the premises. Not until 1879 did it become mandatory to provide a window to every room.

The suburban housing estate on the one hand and the high-density blocks of flats on the other represented the two attempts at a solution produced in England in the latter part of the century. H. J. Dyos estimates that from 1859 to 1867 nearly 37,000 people were displaced from their homes in London by railway development alone. By 1885 the figure had reached 56,000.[5] The Select Committee on Artisans and Labourers Dwellings of 1881 recognized that these were the alternative solutions open. The Committee believed, for reasons of finance, work convenience and family unity, that the poorer class of working man must be housed near his work, but it was generally felt that other members of the working classes

[5] H. J. Dyos, 'Railways and Housing in Victorian London', *Journal of Transport History*, Vol. 2, No. 1 (May 1955).

should live in the suburbs. The adoption of the country villa, earlier
in the century, by the middle classes, as a retreat from the cities,
was compatible with their rationalization of the displacement of the
working population from the central areas, on the grounds that it
was healthier to live in the suburbs and travel into work daily. The
suburban housing estate, from which workmen could commute to
their place of work, opened up a whole new ideology in the development of cities. James Hole, in *Suburban Dwellings and Cheap Railway Fares*,[6] conceded that block dwellings were inevitable as a
means of housing the very poor who had to be near their work, but
for the artisan, a cottage in the suburbs was ideal, as here he could
have a garden and enjoy the pure air. Some of the earliest sup-
porters of block dwellings believed that 'a neat cottage in the middle
of a nice garden . . . was the best type of house for the poor man,
since the garden would keep him occupied, away from the beer-
shop'.[7]

In the second half of the century, ideas for solving the problems
of housing the poor in the expanding cities were related increasingly
to the evil influences of the city and the purity of the countryside.
That these evil influences might spread from the slums was a lurk-
ing menace. The weakness of religion in the city was contrasted
with its strength in the village. The virtues of the countryside were
extolled in literature, while the vice, squalor and evil of the city were
dramatized into a general myth of mystery and sin in cheap
journals. There were political fears of groups of militant workers
involving themselves in revolutionary movements.

In this climate suburbia was born. The middle classes, who had
so energetically helped to create the cities, envisaged the suburban
environment as the working classes' haven from the corruption and
pollution of city dwelling. Arguments put forward for housing
working men in the centre of the city were based purely on practical
necessity, not ideals. This is not to say that no idealistic suggestions were made during the century. Many social reformers
and progressive industrialists, concerned with the general prob-

---

[6] London, 1884.
[7] Quoted in W. V. Hole, 'The Housing of the Working Classes in Britain,
1850-1914', unpublished thesis in the Library of the London School of
Economics.

lems of industrial society, often put their ideas into practice.

Robert Owen was one of the first men to assert that the working and living environment was important to the improvement of industrial conditions. In and around the New Lanark Mills, which he owned, he introduced better pay, shorter hours and better housing for his workers. In 1816 he established an 'Institution for the Formation of Character', which provided educational facilities for children and adults. Children between three and ten were catered for during the day, and older children and adults during the evening. His ideas for dealing with poverty were developed and elaborated in a report presented to the Committee on the Poor Laws. He proposed 'Villages of Unity and Co-operation' of varying population. In his Report to the Committee of the Association for the Relief of the Manufacturing and Labouring Poor, presented to the House of Commons in 1817, he suggested villages of 500-1,500 people; and in his report to the County of Lanark in 1820, villages of 300-2,000. Housing would be arranged around squares containing public buildings and surrounded by 1,000 to 1,500 acres of open space. Three sides of the square would consist of lodging-houses of four rooms each, with a heating and ventilation system, mainly for married couples with up to two children. The fourth side would consist of dormitories for all children exceeding two in a family, or children over three years old. The public buildings would consist of a kitchen and mess-rooms; a building incorporating an infants' school, lecture-room and place of worship; another containing a school for older children, a committee-room and adult library; an infirmary; accommodation for visitors and tree-planted grounds for exercise and recreation. Gardens would surround the housing squares and beyond the gardens would be buildings and space for industry and agriculture.

Robert Owen's proposals formed the first comprehensive, detailed theory of Town Planning in the modern sense. He developed the political and economic premises, the actual building plans and the financial estimate. Unfortunately he antagonized public opinion largely by attributing the miserable condition of men's existence to misconceptions of religious teaching. He was undoubtedly one of the least paternalistic of the nineteenth-century social reformers.

At the same time as Robert Owen was developing his ideas in

England, Charles Fourier was thinking along similar lines in France. In his philosophy, the idea of co-operation in all fields was seen as the way to achieve universal harmony. His 'Ideal City' was a transitional stage towards the goal and would consist of three zones : (1) the main zone, (2) suburbs and main manufactories, (3) avenues and extreme outskirts. The city would be characterized by large houses, plenty of open space, communal accommodation and a concentration of services that would achieve improved human relationships. The later stage in the transition would be based on a rational, functional unit called the 'Phalanx', which would replace the more indeterminate community of the earlier stage, and a single building, the 'Phalanstery', which would replace the city. The Phalanx would house 1,620 people who would co-operate in the cultivation of 5,000 acres of land but would be free to follow their own desires and have rights of private ownership as well.

Later and perhaps more practical examples of planned communities all owe something to the ideas of Owen. In 1849, in the midst of the Anti-Corn Law and the Chartist movements, Edward Ackroyd with his brother established Copley, the first of two planned villages in the neighbourhood of Halifax. Ackroyd was a textile manufacturer and one of the largest employers of labour in the district. Copley was established on land adjoining one of his brother's mills. Ackroyd himself said that the village was 'erected not merely for the purpose of aggregating a sufficient number of operatives for the supply of labour, but also with an eye to the improvement of their social condition, by fitting up their houses with every requisite, comfort and convenience'. He admitted, however, that 'in a financial aspect the Copley experiment is not very successful' and he was not able to achieve much improvement in the planning of the houses, which were still in the back-to-back form typical of the time. In the later village of Ackroydon, begun in 1861, he employed the architect George Gilbert Scott and was able to abandon the back-to-back house and produce an improved dwelling.[8]

In 1853 Sir Titus Salt established a planned estate at Saltaire

[8] See J. L. Berbiers, 'The Planned Villages of Halifax', *Building* (London, July 1966).

near Bradford. Bournville and Port Sunlight are in a sense classic examples of housing estates built by benevolent industrialists to house their workers and belong to the latter part of the century.

Unfortunately these ideas and examples were very small drops in the ocean, and were in effect rural colonies based on schemes unrepeatable on anything like a wide enough scale to make an impact on the total problem. A more extreme and impracticable proposition, for mass emigration, was suggested by General Booth. Events overtook ideas and the solution, if indeed it may be called a solution, was movement into the suburbs coupled with cheap transport. No solution was offered for rehousing in the centre of the cities. No thought was given to possible future problems.

By the end of the century new forms of transport helped to make the development of suburbs even more feasible. Electricity for tramways and the underground railway and internal combustion engines for buses opened up new areas for suburban housing, and vacant spaces between the older suburban railway lines were filled in. Housing did not have to be restricted to walking distance from the railway station when there were trams and buses. Thus the complex pattern of metropolitan transport in large towns all over the industrialized areas of the world was set for several decades. In Western Europe it was set for half a century; in the United States for a shorter period, until the widespread ownership of the motor-car added a further and as yet unresolved problem to urbanization.

Despite the headlong plunge into suburbia which took place as a result of the Victorian attitude to the city and its problems, the ideas of Robert Owen and other pioneers of town planning did bear fruit, in the theory put forward by Ebenezer Howard in 1898 in his book *To-Morrow: A Peaceful Path to Real Reform* (later renamed *Garden Cities of To-Morrow*). Ironically, the practical application of Howard's ideas has, with a few notable exceptions, helped to form the pattern of the twentieth-century suburb throughout the world. Yet Howard was essentially anti-suburban. The core of his thesis was that the size of towns was something that could and should be controlled in relation to industry, agriculture and all the other activities necessary to a whole community. It is in this sense that he lies in a direct line of descent from Robert Owen. In his introduction to a new edition of Howard's book, Lewis Mumford

wrote that it 'has done more than any other single book to guide
the modern town planning movement and to alter its objectives'.
He noted also that Howard was in the tradition of a group of early
nineteenth-century writers as well as later thinkers such as Henry
George and Peter Kropotkin. He added with great emphasis that
'The Garden City, as Howard defined it, is not a suburb but the
antithesis of a suburb; not a mere rural retreat, but a more integrated foundation for an effective urban life.'[9]

The essential features of Howard's conception of a Garden City
are that it should be a complete and integrated social unit with a
limited population and controlled growth; that there should be
communal ownership of land and participation in the profits that
would accrue from increased land values; that there should be a
permanent reserve of agricultural land, both to encourage local
food production and to create a pleasant environment. The total
area should be 6,000 acres, of which only 1,000 would be absorbed
by built-up areas. The distinctive features of this plan were the
provision of a central area of civic buildings, surrounded successively
by a circle of parkland, a glass-enclosed arcade, rings of houses and
gardens, a ring of industries and workshops, a circle railway and
finally agricultural land. The population of the city would be
32,000. In a chapter of his book entitled 'Social Cities' Howard
sets down his notion of the correct principle of a city's growth,
which in many ways has had the most significant impact on later
planning theory. The idea is that once a garden city had grown to
its limit of 32,000 people, further growth should be channelled into
the establishment of another similar city, separated by a rural belt
but connected by a system of rapid transit (it is interesting that
Howard uses this term), and then another, so that in course of time
there would be a cluster of cities around a central city, rather larger
than the garden cities, with a population of 58,000.

Here, of course, is the blueprint for the satellite town which was
used first in England and later in Scandinavia, France and the
United States as a means of providing for the expansion of large
cities, although what has been built so far has been the satellite part
of the idea rather than the cluster. Howard's concept was still very

[9] Ebenezer Howard, *Garden Cities of To-Morrow*, edited by F. J. Osborn
with an Introduction by Lewis Mumford (London: Faber & Faber, 1945).

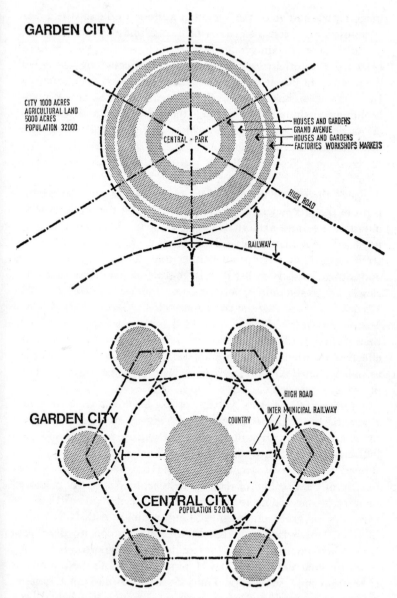

GARDEN CITY

CITY 1000 ACRES
AGRICULTURAL LAND
5000 ACRES
POPULATION 32000

CENTRAL · PARK

HOUSES AND GARDENS
GRAND AVENUE
HOUSES AND GARDENS
FACTORIES WORKSHOPS MARKETS

HIGH ROAD

RAILWAY

GARDEN CITY

COUNTRY

HIGH ROAD
INTER MUNICIPAL RAILWAY

CENTRAL CITY
POPULATION 52000

FIG. I   Ebenezer Howard's Garden City and its relationship to a cluster of cities

much representative of the Victorian attitude to the city as a place of industrial and social squalor which could only be regenerated by a healthy dose of countryside. The twentieth-century garden suburb is far from his original conception and is ineffective in coping with the problem of housing a growing urban population. The totality of Howard's ideas has been largely ignored and only today are we beginning to think seriously about the possibilities and desirability of 'participation' by people as a whole in the control and development of their surroundings.

Towards the end of the nineteenth century there was also a movement in the arts generally which reacted against the products of the industrial age and against its effects on man. This was the movement led by William Morris. Here again we find an attitude which tends towards the countryside rather than the city, to rural crafts and cottage industry rather than large-scale industry, and to smaller, closely knit communities, very much self-sufficient in the sense that Ebenezer Howard saw the community of the Garden City. William Morris was more directly concerned with practical construction than was Howard, and, together with the architect Philip Webb, he effectively started a style in domestic architecture which has been as much abused in later periods as were Howard's ideas of town planning.

Significantly the two joined forces. Morris started a rather Romantic but nonetheless functional 'cottage' style of architecture for houses, which drew upon medieval sources for form and used indigenous and natural materials in a direct and simple way. This formed the basis of architectural style for most of the garden suburbs of the first half of the twentieth century and it degenerated more or less according to the financial or social status of those for whom the suburbs were intended. Once again, as with Howard, the ideas of Morris have not only been misunderstood by those who have seized upon his forms, but quite simply ignored. Something in the approach of Morris and Howard appealed to the aspirations of the growing middle class. Probably it had to do with the desire to emulate country gentlemen, with rural values, which had been praised so much and for so long. The cottage style of house com-

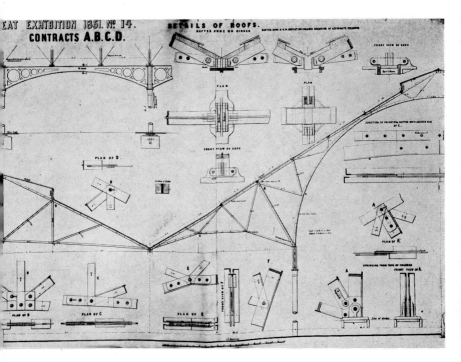

king drawing by Joseph Paxton for the Great Exhibition, 1851.

es van der Rohe: Court House perspective drawing.

William Morris

I. K. Brunel

bined with the garden suburb estate offered the nearest thing to rustic gentility the majority of this growing class could achieve, and ultimately it has become the ideal not only for them but also for an increasingly affluent section of the working class.

I began my brief survey of the Victorian age and its legacies with a consideration of the effects of technology, the later development of which has been of enormous significance in the twentieth century. I have already mentioned the appearance of the motor-car. In a more direct architectural sense, the development of steel combined with electricity as a source of power, when confronted with the pressure for space in city centres, made possible the idea of the skyscraper. For this building form a very strong structural material was needed, combined with a means of vertical transport. Perhaps this is an oversimplification of what happened in Chicago in the 1880s and 1890s. Nevertheless, in essence this was the situation.

Although this new building form was used first for commercial purposes, its potential was recognized even in those early days, for hotels, multi-purpose buildings and apartment blocks. The new structural concept of this form was the skeleton frame. Previously such a form had been restricted to basically single-storey buildings like station sheds and exhibition halls. Multi-storey buildings were generally of masonry construction, with cast-iron columns used internally to open up the space as much as possible for factories and offices. But the height of such buildings was severely limited. The skeleton frame allowed a continuity of structure, combined with a relative lightness in weight, so that not only could buildings be built higher safely, but massive external walls with limited openings were no longer necessary. The external wall could be glass.

William le Baron Jenney was the founder of what has become known as the 'Chicago School' of architects, which includes many names famous in the history of the origins of modern architecture. The development of this school coincided with the boom years of Chicago's industrial and commercial development as the great business centre of the United States. Of this school the art historian, Giedion, has written :

The architects of the Chicago school employed a new type of construction : the iron skeleton. At that time it was called quite

B

simply 'Chicago construction'. They invented a new kind of foundation to cope with the problem of the muddy ground of Chicago : the floating foundation. They introduced the horizontally elongated window : the Chicago window.

They created the modern business and administration building. The importance of the school for the history of architecture lies in this fact : for the first time in the nineteenth century the schism between construction and architecture, between the engineer and the architect, was healed.[10]

Perhaps, after all, Robert Jordan's statement, 'the main contribution of the Victorian age to architecture is the slum', is not entirely justifiable, although he was writing specifically about the British scene. Yet in physical terms, in volume of building, in the immediate effect on cities both then and since, this summing-up may well be accurate. However, in the realm of ideas, in attitudes towards urbanization, just as important has been the idea of the suburb, in all its implications, and the garden suburb in particular. Equally important to later generations have been the technological developments I have just described. In addition, motor transport has added a new dimension to the problems of urbanization in the second half of our century. But also of immense importance was the acknowledgment late in the nineteenth century that some degree of planning, of conscious interference in the so-called natural growth of cities, and in their problems, was not only possible, but even desirable.

[10] Siegfried Giedion, *Space Time and Architecture* (Cambridge, Mass.: Harvard University Press, 1954).

Chapter 2

The Age of the Suburb: 1900-1939

The relationship of technical innovation to the environment of a developing industrial society, and the reactions of professional men —administrators, politicians and reformers—to the problems of this changing society, have been discussed. By the end of the nineteenth century no satisfactory solution to the central problems of urbanization had been found. The twentieth century inherited these problems together with a number of new techniques that had been developed in the closing years of the nineteenth century. These techniques marked the opening of a new phase in the process of industrialization. Together with this came a new phase in the urbanization of industrial society.

For most of the nineteenth century steam had been the basic source of power and coal the basic fuel. The end of the century saw the introduction of a new, widening range of fuels and sources of power. First came gas as a by-product of coal, then electricity, and finally oil. The combination of electricity and oil in the invention of the internal combustion engine eventually re-established the road as the primary means of communication by land. Gas and electricity revolutionized the domestic scene. New forms of communication, the telegraph and the telephone, the invention of the typewriter, made possible the enormous expansion of commercial activity. Combined with the new sources of power, this in turn made possible a greater freedom in the location of industry. Henceforth regions and countries, which hitherto had been mainly agricultural and unsuitable for large-scale industry, could take part in the process of industrialization.

Industrialization also began to mean not principally heavy industry, but more and more the mass production of everyday articles

35

and the development of new products springing from new techniques, sources of power and communications. The expansion of commercial activity and the development of 'consumer' industries were accompanied by considerable social changes. There was a growing lower-middle class of men and women, engaged in the expanding commercial activities. Pressure and agitation for social reform on the political level, swinging away from the middle-class philanthropists, were being led by a politically organized working class, which, in Britain, was gaining political power through constitutional means. Elsewhere the achievement of power by the working class was accompanied by violence and revolution. In all spheres of social life, in science, in the arts, there were powerful forces of change at work.

In the process of urbanization this was the period of the great suburban explosion, particularly in those cities most affected by the expansion of commerce and industry—London in particular. In the years preceding the First World War there was tremendous growth in the development of working-class and lower-middle-class suburbs, which was closely linked to the development of new forms of transport. In 1902 and 1907 cheap transport facilities in London were examined by the Browning Hall Conference.[1] It was reported that over the five-year period there had been a substantial increase in all forms of transport. Underground and surface electric railways and trams had spread rapidly but unevenly. A considerable movement of population had taken place and those affected were accommodated in small houses built by speculators on relatively cheap land some distance from central London. The London County Council, through the Board of Trade, continually pressed for the extension of cheap workmen's fares on public transport. In 1908, 28 million passengers travelled by train in London on workmen's tickets.

The housing policy of the London County Council was closely linked to these developments. An LCC report in 1908 (Present Aspects of the Housing Question) stated: '. . . the operation has retained in central districts working-class populations which might

[1] Referred to in W. V. Hole, 'The Housing of the Working Classes in Britain, 1850-1914'. See also *Royal Commission on London Traffic, 1905-1906.*

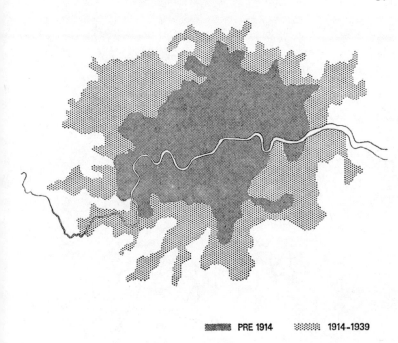

PRE 1914   1914-1939

FIG. 2   London suburban development 1914-39

have been far more cheaply accommodated in the suburbs, while
the sites on which they were housed have been shut out from their
natural commercial development. The class whose hours of work
preclude living in the suburbs [i.e. the lowest paid workers] is a
small minority'. The LCC assumed that the outward movement of
population represented the desires of the people themselves and
stated that it was useless to oppose it. Housing policy was therefore
conveniently directed towards accommodating the movement. While
some thought was given to the hope that the suburbs would become
reasonably balanced communities, none was given to the ultimate
effect of large areas of central London becoming exclusively commercial. The old uncontrolled pattern of city growth was being
encouraged for economic reasons despite all the problems which,
with a little more thought, could have been foreseen. The improved

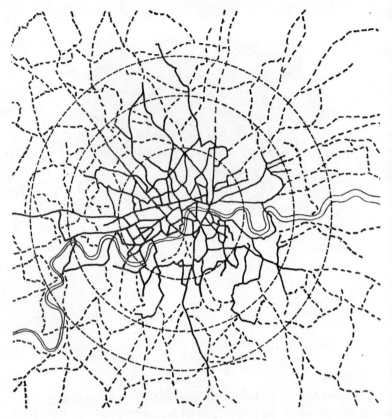

FIG. 3   London Transport bus routes before 1900 and at 1930 (broken lines)

means of transport both accelerated the growth and spread the urban area farther and farther from the city centre.

It is true that even in 1900, when the suburban sprawl was still of comparatively low density, there were some people who thought that this tendency should be averted. Unfortunately their alternatives were not exactly progressive and were out of tune with the social movement of the times. A group of architects put forward the view that high buildings were the only way of housing the poor decently and that local by-laws, preventing the erection of such buildings,

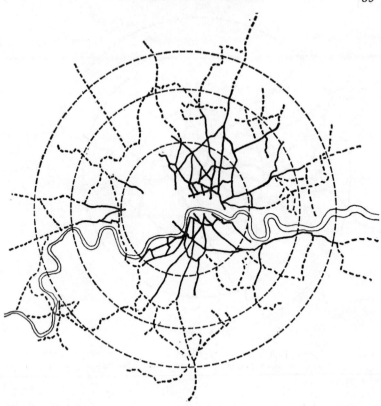

FIG. 4   London Transport tram routes before 1900 and at 1930 (broken lines)

were thoroughly deplorable. They admitted that this method had so far failed as a means of rehousing the slums, but thought that this could be remedied by adapting the design more carefully to the mode of life of the poor. They particularly approved a recent change in the policy of housing societies which involved the abandonment of the practice of including bathrooms in workers' dwellings. They were most concerned that rigid economy should be the first aim.[2] Their attitude might be thought wildly reactionary and typical of

[2] See Honeyman, Spalding, Wallace and Fleming, 'Working Class Dwellings', *RIBA Journal*, Vol. 7, No. 11 (1900), 249-50.

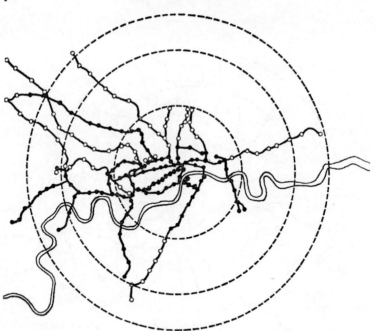

FIG. 5 London Transport underground railway lines before 1900 (black junctions) and at 1930 (white junctions). Note the major development to the north-west.

its time. Unhappily the same attitude is prevalent in official circles all over the world today. The idea that cutting costs and building more houses more cheaply will solve the housing problem is a popular current myth.

While the new suburbs provided better standards of light, air and open space than the more densely built-up central areas, the improvements in living conditions were largely marginal. The communities did not become balanced, as the LCC so piously hoped. They remained largely one-class communities. Shops, schools and other facilities were provided as they developed, but they were basically dormitory suburbs, the working populations of which migrated each day into central London. Architecturally they were dreary. The enormous scale of the developments, their monotonous regularity and their meanness created a subhuman environment which was only relieved over the years by the few trees and bits of green which managed to survive the monstrous sprawl.

The transport services which made these new suburbs feasible had not yet become fully economical. Only after 1910, when motor-buses began to supplement and then replace the trams, could the catchment-areas at the earlier extremities of the underground lines be extended sufficiently to provide an economic volume of pas-sengers.

The principle of suburban development following the pattern of transport was never so clearly demonstrated as by Frank Pick, head of London Transport, in the years after the First World War.[3] He fully appreciated the need for co-ordinated road services as an extension of the underground railway. Underground railways and bus routes were extended into open country in the expectation that suburban development would make them remunerative. This policy succeeded, sometimes to an embarrassing extent. On this basis, West, North-West, and South London were developed between the two wars and the process was only halted in 1939. This was the second suburban explosion in London, planned only to the extent that transport authorities could see their role as catalysts and used their power in a developing situation.

The old attitude of the London County Council towards de-centralization of the working population went hand in hand with the transport policy. At the same time, after the First World War the LCC started to take a more active part in building and develop-ment. It was only as a result of the housing shortage after the war and changing attitudes towards government responsibility in hous-ing that local authorities began to use powers which they had pos-sessed since the mid-nineteenth century to build houses for renting. While the LCC had been the first authority to undertake housing schemes before the war, those had been restricted to slum rehousing in central London.

In 1919 the LCC embarked upon the building of the largest housing estate in the world, which, when completed in 1935, housed 90,000 people. The estate was planned to meet the bulk of London's urgent housing needs and, in particular to provide new homes for

[3] F. Pick, 'Growth and Form in Modern Cities', *Journal of the Institute of Transport*, Vol. 8 (1926).

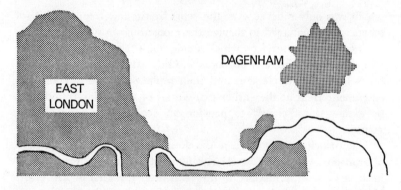

FIG. 6   Dagenham in relation to East London

people from the East End which contained, as the Council stated, 'the most densely occupied and the most overcrowded areas, and generally the worst conditions in London. . . . The natural and necessary outlet was in an easterly direction from London, and the dense development in the intervening outer London districts (built in the pre-war period) made it necessary to go as far as Becontree to obtain an estate of a size sufficient for the requirements'.[4] Dagenham was planned as an estate of 24,000 houses in a five-year programme after 1919. The programme was extended partly for economic reasons, and partly by changes in government policy. In a survey carried out in 1958-9 by Peter Willmott, the problems resulting from planning of this sort were studied. Willmott, in setting out his reasons for choosing to study Dagenham, states : 'A third reason for the choice of Dagenham was that it is, in terms of town planning, such a monstrosity. Its design and layout offend most of the canons of urban planning, and it is commonly held up, among planners and architects, as a dreadful warning—a supreme illustration of how not to build a new community. Here, if anywhere, one might see how planning mistakes had warped the social life of a community.'[5]

[4] LCC Minutes, Housing Committee Report (June 22, 1926).
[5] Peter Willmott, *The Evolution of a Community* (London: Routledge & Kegan Paul, 1963).

The survey found that although most people were reasonably content to live in Dagenham, it was almost exclusively a one-class community. It lacked social facilities and there was considerable educational disadvantage for children, since it offered neither a strong cultural background nor any educational ambition on the part of the parents. There were social and economic pressures against the child who wanted to stay on at school and go to university. Political interest was low—Dagenham still has one of the lowest percentage polls in the country at elections. This suggests that in a period when there is a housing shortage, as at the time the survey was carried out (there was at least as great a shortage as in 1919), people will be glad to live anywhere they can find a reasonable house. And they will make the best of their environment whatever the inherent disadvantages. The end result is sad in human terms and is an indictment of short-sighted and economically biased attitudes.

Another important factor that led to suburban expansion in London was the changing location of industry. This was closely linked to transport changes and to the possibilities we have outlined in the new sources of power. Pressure on land in central areas from commercial interests provided the impetus for industry to move outwards and the newer consumer industries established themselves in the suburban belt. The industrial developments along the new arterial roads in the West and North-West of London are particular examples of this trend.

The population increase in the region as a whole was the basic cause of the growth of London. There was a natural increase which was responsible for over 60 per cent of the rise in population between 1921 and 1931, but in addition there was a migration of people into the London area. It is interesting to note that in the period 1921-39, while the population of Greater London increased from 7.5 million to 8.7 million, the population of central London (the administrative county of London) fell by over 446,000. This gives some idea of the scale of suburban growth. The social structure of suburban life is summed up by James H. Johnson :

Since most of the building around London was constructed by private speculative builders, the majority of those people who

eventually came to live in outer London were selected by their
ability to put down a deposit and meet regular mortgage payments; but they also passed through a demographic filter. For
many people the desire for a semi-detached house with a garden
cannot have manifested itself until their family included a young
child. As a result of both these factors, the typical family moving
into a new suburban estate was a lower middle class couple in
their late twenties or early thirties, with one or two children.
The quality of suburban living was largely conditioned by the
resultant structure of population and society.[6]

One of the most significant newcomers on the urban scene in the
1930s was the private car. In view of the historic interaction between city and communication pattern, and more particularly the
acceptance of suburbia as a remedy for the growth of the city, the
coming of motor transport was significant in many ways. Transport
of materials by road, together with the new fuels and sources of
power, made possible the decentralization of industry, and particularly light manufacturing industry which did so much to enlarge
the consumer market. Bus transport enabled new suburbs to be
built around the new industrial areas so that commuting patterns
in, for example, the suburban and industrial areas of North-West
London, became tangential rather than radial. Workers could now
live in the suburbs and be near their place of work. So the lighter
manufacturing industries which had hitherto been housed in central
areas moved out and made way for the physical, allied to the commercial, expansion of banks, insurance companies, distribution,
financial and administrative offices that accompanied the extension
of the consumer industries. The pattern of commuting to the centre
underwent a social change : now the commuters were upper-middle-
class businessmen as before, together with a very much enlarged
lower-middle-class 'white collar' group of (workers. The manual
workers almost disappeared and so, eventually, did the working
men's cheap fares, almost without a murmur. This change was
spread over about two generations.

[6] James H. Johnson, 'Suburban Expansion of Housing in London' from
Greater London, edited by J. T. Coppock and Hugh C. Prince (London:
Faber & Faber, 1964).

The growing importance of road transport, which had been over-shadowed by the railways since the early nineteenth century, was evident in the construction of radial 'arterial' roads in many cities and of ring roads or bypasses around others. Generally the purpose of these new roads was to service the new decentralized industries, as for example the Great West Road, Western Avenue and Eastern Avenue in London. Along these roads speculative housing was built in 'ribbons' not more than a few streets in depth on either side. This 'ribbon development', as it became known, was a general pattern of suburban development in the 1930s. Only gradually were the spaces between the ribbons filled up, in the same way as with the suburban railways in the nineteenth century. This evolution bore no relation to the social needs or functions of the community beyond easing travel to and from work. It was one of the factors which post-Second World War town planning legislation sought to avoid.

This was the process by which suburbia and suburban life came about in London. The pattern was followed in many other cities, particularly in the United States and those parts of the world where industrialization and commercial expansion were taking place, although the details and situations may have varied from city to city.

Meanwhile, in the fields of architecture, design and planning, what appeared to be a major revolution was occurring. In the long term this has had a great impact on the design of the environment. At the time and, indeed, up to the Second World War, its influence was limited mainly to artistic and intellectual circles, and it had very little effect on the suburban explosion. On the other hand, new construction techniques and new materials had a strong influence on the buildings most closely connected with industry and com-merce. In this sense there was a direct parallel with what had hap-pened in the early years of the nineteenth century.

In the first chapter I described briefly the birth of the skeleton-framed building in Chicago in the 1880s. A little later, in France, reinforced concrete—a combination of the tensile strength of steel with the compressive strength of concrete—was invented. With reinforced concrete, skeleton-framed structures could be built in a similar way to steel ones, but with much less steel. This was of considerable significance to countries which were not steel producers. The large-scale building associated with mass-production processes and expanding commercial activity could be done in regions and countries that were only now becoming industrialized.

Out of the American and European experience came more or less parallel movements in architecture which eventually merged. In Europe, out of the movement led first by Pugin and later by William Morris and Ruskin in England, there grew an attitude to design based upon crafts and craftsmanship, with an idea that the truly functional artifacts could be beautiful without embellishment. At first the movement developed a style : in France and England *Art Nouveau*, in Germany the *Jugendstil*. And out of these roots grew the Bauhaus in Germany. In France the pioneer of reinforced concrete design, the architect Auguste Perret, nurtured in his atelier a group of young architects, with one man head and shoulders above the rest—Le Corbusier. In Chicago in the late nineteenth century the most powerful architect was Louis Sullivan, and under his wing grew the talent of another master, Frank Lloyd Wright. The influence of the Bauhaus, of Le Corbusier and of Lloyd Wright, has been paramount in the development of modern architecture. At the same time the importance of their roots cannot be underestimated, particularly if one is to try to make an objective assessment of where their influence has led.

Since we have hitherto been much concerned with urbanization, it would be most appropriate first to consider Le Corbusier, who, of these influential masters, has had the greatest influence on planning. He was, perhaps, the first great architect to concern himself deeply with the social problems of architecture and urbanism and to put forward some sort of universal scheme in the way that earlier social reformers had done. In this sense he was the first truly modern architect. Lloyd Wright, Gropius and Mies van der Rohe concerned themselves with some aspects of the problem, but their main work was concentrated in the same social spheres in which the nineteenth-century architects had worked, namely among middle-class and commercial patronage.

In 1923 Le Corbusier published *La Ville Radieuse*, in which he set out his ideas on town planning. They incorporated the basic

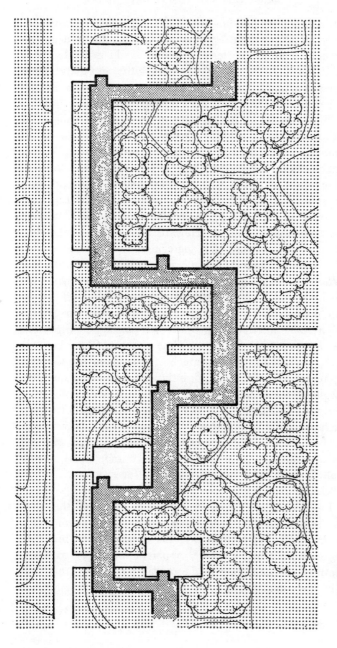

Dwelling Unities   ⊐⊏ **Vehicular Routes**   **Pedestrian Areas**

FIG. 7 Le Corbusier's 'La Ville Radieuse', showing the separation of vehicular and pedestrian routes related to housing.

concept of high-density building which left large areas of land free, to be developed as parkland, so that the city would be a garden city in the real sense of the term. Housing would generally be in low, multi-storey buildings in linear form with right-angle bends and forming courtyards or vast outdoor rooms, with the ground floor left open so that one could walk through from space to space. Office buildings would be in the form of tall towers, while other public institutions—schools, health centres, libraries—would consist of low buildings set in the parklike squares. Corbusier was one of the first planners to acknowledge the impact of motor transport and his plans show provision for motorways and service roads very clearly articulated and with clear separation of pedestrian and vehicular areas. As Jane Jacobs has pointed out, his basic concept was in the tradition of Ebenezer Howard and incorporated many of the social assumptions and segregation of functions that Howard's planning includes.[7] There is a clearly utopian ring about La Ville Radieuse which fails to take into account the dynamism of modern industrial society. Nevertheless, it was the first serious attempt to provide a form for large-scale planning in modern terms, with a viable alternative to traditional housing concepts. His ideas were not put into practice until the 1950s in Chandigarh in East Punjab, India. Even though much of it is operative, Chandigarh is still under construction and it is difficult to assess its qualities. In the first place, the social situation of India is very different from that of Europe, and there is a level of social segregation which would not be acceptable in Europe. This finds clear expression in the physical structure of the city of Chandigarh. The pressures of transport and industry hardly exist in terms we understand, so that it is virtually impossible to compare it with, for example, the new towns in Britain.

In La Ville Radieuse Corbusier produced many of the ideas which have influenced later generations of architects and planners, and while his works on architecture, the design of the buildings themselves, may have had a greater apparent impact on architecture, his intrinsic influence lies in the overall picture he created of buildings in their urban setting. It is also interesting that his was

[7] Jane Jacobs, The Death and Life of Great American Cities (New York: Random House, 1961).

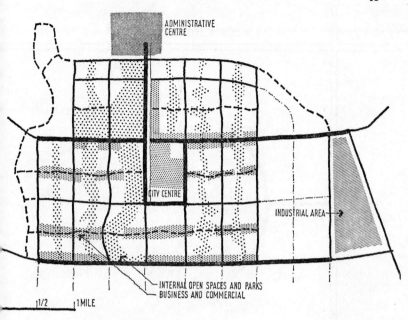

FIG. 8   Le Corbusier: plan of Chandigarh

the European approach to the city in contrast to Frank Lloyd
Wright's ideas. Lloyd Wright originally published a project for what
he called 'Broadacre City' in 1934, developing his ideas between
then and 1958. His concepts were perhaps more consciously in the
Ebenezer Howard tradition than those of Corbusier, but represented
the fully suburban concept, possible only in terms of the larger
available space and the more widespread ownership of the motor-
car typical in the United States. The social implications of his plans
seem rather sinister to the European mind. He set out clearly defined areas for 'minimum houses', 'medium houses' and 'larger
houses', apparently quite unaware of the inferences of so doing. In
later town planning projects of limited scope he used the road as
an architectural feature, but there is a bombast and naïveté in his
schemes which make them of little value in any serious consideration
of the problems.

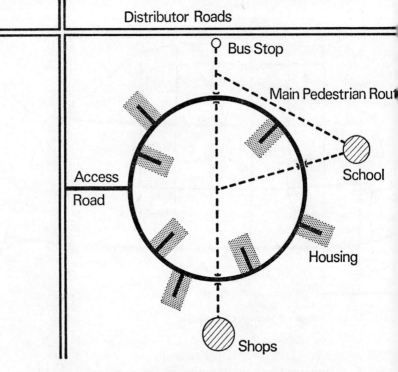

FIG. 9   Radburn planning: diagram indicating the principles of vehicular and pedestrian separation.

On the other hand, one of the very important developments in town planning related to transport was the development of what has become known as 'Radburn' planning. Radburn, sited in New Jersey and planned by Clarence Stein in 1929, was a garden city conception in the tradition of Ebenezer Howard. Its importance lay in traffic control, in segregation of vehicular and pedestrian traffic in residential areas.

Returning to Corbusier, there was a field of urban design where he had an opportunity, in Europe, to develop his ideas. He moved towards the concept of a single building providing all the basic living requirements of a community, and called it a 'Unité d'habitation'. This was a high-rise building with dwellings, each of which was on more than one level, each having a large open terrace, access by means of internal 'streets' rather than corridors, with floors containing shops and other facilities, and with a nursery school and terraces on the roof. The theoretical origin of this idea can be traced back to Charles Fourier and his 'Phalanstery', noted earlier on. Corbusier's first 'Unité d'habitation' was built in Marseilles in the 1950s and was followed by another at Nantes. His idea, and even more his architectural interpretation, deeply influenced a generation of young architects at the time, and are reflected in a range of buildings and projects designed by the then London County Council Architects' Department. His architectural ideas were also apparent in the so-called 'Brutalist' movement that began in the 1950s. In a consciously sculptural way, he gave reinforced concrete, the main material utilized for his buildings, a deliberate rough finish. Corbusier was a painter as well as sculptor. Striving for universality in a romantic, philosophic manner, he developed a theory of proportion called 'Le Modulor', to which he related all his work and for which he claimed a universal application. He was very much a romantic artist, a visionary and an experimentalist, but with roots firmly in the nineteenth-century tradition, similar to the cubist painters. However much he said about functionalism, and his notorious phrase concerning the house as a 'machine for living in' was one of the most provocative elements in the battle for modern architecture, there is a very real sense in which his buildings are not so much functional as works of sculpture. They cannot, on the whole, be accepted as general solutions to the problems of modern urban society, however much they may be admired and emulated by lesser men. They are architectural monuments of great importance. They helped and led architects to rid themselves of much of the accumulated dross of the past and demonstrated the possibilities of a new approach. But they were of an age and attitude which had not yet appreciated the full implications of life in an industrialized society, and one may be forgiven for thinking of the works of Corbusier and his contemporaries as the swan-song of a long Romantic movement in architecture, containing within it the seeds of the future, but a future very different to the one they had envisaged.

About his contemporaries one might say the same, only more so. Frank Lloyd Wright worked in the American mid-West, in wide-open prairie country. His houses were almost exclusively for wealthy businessmen. Space was no problem, and Lloyd Wright set out to conquer architectural space in a new way, appropriate to the land-scape and the booming self-assured society in which he worked. His attempts at solutions to the wider problems of housing either re-quired too much land to make them generally applicable, or else were so wildly bombastic, as in his mile-high centre, as to be rightly dismissed as unrealistic fantasies. Lloyd Wright's life spanned a considerable period, but he was essentially a man of the pre-First World War period. He was highly idiosyncratic, romantic, an inspired and dedicated artist-craftsman. Like Corbusier, whose work he dis-liked, he helped architects to see in a new way, to appreciate the potentials of the materials they could use and of the new techniques at their disposal.

In terms of modern technology, it is probably Mies van der Rohe who, of the masters of the Modern movement in architecture, has had the widest impact. He has worked consistently in the new materials of the age, relying very much on the technology of glass and steel combined in classically pure forms and with a simplicity that few other architects can or dare attempt. The concept of a building clothed in steel and glass was his, and this idea has been taken up almost universally and used with varying degrees of success in appropriate and inappropriate situations. Rather naturally for this form of building, the majority of the major works of Mies and his more successful as well as less successful imitators has been in the field of commercial building, mainly office blocks.

Mies van der Rohe was head of the Bauhaus after Walter Gropius, and the influence of these men and the school of design which they ran has been of great importance, not only in the development of modern architecture, but in the field of design generally and industrial design and graphics in particular. To sum up the work of the Bauhaus in a paragraph or so would be im-possible. I have already noted its roots in the craft tradition. It set out to develop these crafts in relation to modern industrial technol-ogy using new materials and techniques, not to imitate styles of the past but to create a new tradition. Many of the items of furniture which were designed in the late 'twenties and early 'thirties in the Bauhaus have become classical pieces which are still in production. The current taste in furniture design is highly derivative of the forms developed at the Bauhaus, particularly the use of steel tubular construction combined with leather upholstery and glass table-tops. But the influence went deeper and further than this, or than any other specific examples would indicate. The Bauhaus developed a new direction in art and design education which completely cut across the old Beaux-Arts traditions. Contemporary architectural design and art education owe a great deal to the work of the Bauhaus, and probably it is upon these fields that its effect has been strongest. Its educational principles were based on a common approach for all designers, a combination of theory or abstract work and practical application, with great concern for techniques and technology. It was essentially not imitative in the way classical art and design education had been. We tend to take its principles so much for granted today that it is easy to forget how stale and stereotyped had been most art education before the Bauhaus.

Imitative architecture was the norm in the 1930s, a natural reflection of classical, imitative, architectural training. The breeze of modernism—functionalism and so on—was felt, but only allowed to blow away the more ornate frills of false classicism. So there were 'Egyptian' cinemas, town halls with metal-framed windows, even corner windows, and emaciated classical columns—neo-Georgian, with vaguely modern overtones and notably bad proportions—numerous imitations of Stockholm Town Hall, and in Mussolini's Italy and Hitler's Germany the most bombastic, bastardized examples of neo-classical architecture imaginable. In the early days of the Soviet Union modern architecture was welcomed and encouraged, and leading modernists from abroad, including Corbusier, together with an indigenous school of constructivist architects, designed imaginative, exciting buildings. But this did not last long. Under Stalin the Soviet Union went neo-classicist in as bombastic a way as Germany under the Nazis, the argument being that the palaces of past ages were now the palaces of the people, and the new buildings should also be palaces of the kind that the people could understand. There were, of course, deeper dialectic arguments.

It is not easy to sum up this period. First and foremost, the suburban explosion was haphazard, manifested by buildings of poor aesthetic quality, but at the same time a revolution in architecture and design was developing together with a range of new ideas in the field of town planning. Though too late to affect the spread of the suburbs before the Second World War to any marked extent, the revolution of thought, and particularly in design education, had sufficient impact after the war to establish the precepts of modern architecture and planning on a widely accepted basis. The battle had not been won, and is not yet won, but there is now a strategy related to the problems of our time which had not existed in the past.

Chapter 3

Planning and the Welfare State

The first step towards an official planning policy in Britain was the publication in 1943 of Forshaw and Abercrombie's *County of London Plan* followed in 1944 by Abercrombie's *Greater London Plan*. These plans, prepared for the London County Council, laid down the guidelines for the rebuilding of bombed areas and the redevelopment and expansion that were expected to be necessary after the war. The first of the plans looked in detail at the problems of the administrative County of London and made proposals for the zoning of functions in different areas, for transport improvements, and for the rebuilding of the worst bombed residential areas and the City. The second plan looked at the problems of the region as a whole and proposed that the growth of London should be contained by a 'green belt' in which building would be restricted, and that expansion should be channelled into a ring of 'satellite towns' built beyond the green belt. They represented an attempt to apply the planning principles of Ebenezer Howard on a large scale and to an existing situation rather than to a totally new one. Howard's influence was far-reaching, both in the idea of zoning different functions and that of residential neighbourhood units, but perhaps most significantly in the concept of satellite towns on the periphery of a green belt. Even the proposed size of these towns was closely related to Howard's suggestion of a population of 32,000.

The plans described four major defects of London: traffic congestion, depressed housing, inadequacy and maldistribution of open space, and indiscriminate mixed development of industry and housing. The *County of London Plan* attempted to 'strike a balance between contending interests, between different aspects of town activity, no less than between the needs and functions of different sections of the community'. A survey was prepared and London was considered (a) as a community where people live, work and play, (b) as a metropolis—the seat of government, a cultural and commercial centre, (c) as a machine, particularly in relation to transport. Certain important assumptions were made : that no new industry should be admitted to London or the Home Counties; that in accordance with a recommended density of 136 persons to the acre, accommodation for 618,000 people should be provided outside the overcrowded area of the LCC and that to this should be added a further 415,000 from overcrowded areas outside the LCC area, making a total of 1,033,000 persons to be decentralized; that the population of the London area would not increase; that the importance of the Port of London would continue in relation to foreign ports; that new powers of planning, including the control of land values, would become available. The plan was based upon four rings, again owing something to Howard's influence : an Inner Ring, a Suburban Ring, a Green Belt Ring and an Outer Country Ring, the latter to be the main reception area for decentralized population. Included were detailed studies of the structure of the plan, communications, open space, public services and the problems of realization.

In the event a number of the assumptions have proved to be wrong, for one reason or another. The south-east of England and the London area in particular have become the most powerful magnet for commercial and industrial development and, as a result, the population of the region has not remained constant at the 1945 level. Planning powers became available, but control of land values has never been effective. The densities of housing under the planning legislation have never achieved an average in central London of 136 persons per acre, but have been lower. The resultant pressures from the effects of these false assumptions together with an increase in private car ownership, never envisaged by the planners, have inevitably nullified many of the anticipated benefits of the plans.

The proposals made in the *Greater London Plan* were the first to be given legal effect. Under the post-war Labour Government, and as part of its broad policies by which the so-called Welfare State was established, a New Towns Commission was appointed.

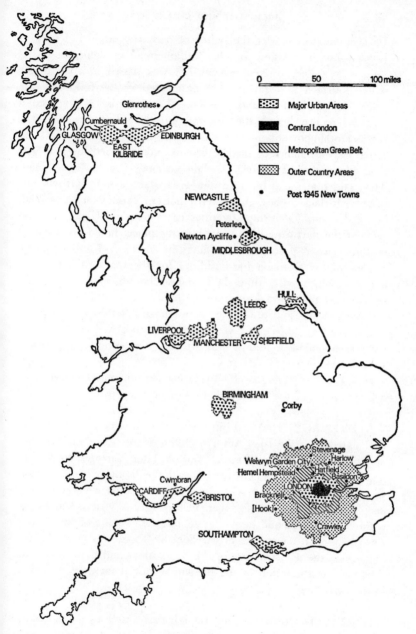

Glenrothes

Cumbernauld
GLASGOW   EDINBURGH
EAST
KILBRIDE

NEWCASTLE

Peterlee
Newton Aycliffe
MIDDLESBROUGH

HULL

LEEDS

LIVERPOOL
MANCHESTER   SHEFFIELD

BIRMINGHAM   Corby

Stevenage
Welwyn Garden City   Harlow
Hemel Hempstead   Hatfield   Basildon
Cwmbran   LONDON
CARDIFF   BRISTOL   Bracknell
[Hook]
Crawley
SOUTHAMPTON

FIG. 10   New Towns and London planning rings

Its task was to consider the policy of decentralization not only in London but in relation to other urban areas, or conurbations as they were called. A New Towns Act was passed in 1946 under which fourteen new towns were designated in the following five years, ten of them around London. The Commission prepared a series of reports before the Act was passed, setting out clearly a number of important social needs which should be satisfied. They stated that a balance of income groups and of varied interests was desirable and that one-class neighbourhoods should be avoided. They said that social life in a new town starts afresh, but will not necessarily lack vigour. A standard pattern cannot be prescribed, but a demand for certain facilities can be assumed and must be met. At the start a multi-purpose meeting-place should be provided in the form of permanent buildings in advance of full demand. Suggestions were made for buildings for theatre, music, the arts and for dance-halls; that there should be an adequate library service, and that special attention be paid to places of refreshment, including hotels and a variety of restaurants, teashops and cafés. Play-space for children and young people and various club facilities were recommended, and it was stressed that community centres should cater for all age groups.

How much of this was effectively carried out may be seen from a brief survey of the first generation of new towns.

STEVENAGE (Hertfordshire) was the first new town to be designated after the 1946 Act. An area of 6,100 acres was specified and the planned population was 60,000, later increased to 80,000. The aim was for low density; most of the living accommodation was to be of two storeys, with few flats. Neighbourhoods of 10,000 people were devised, having their own centres as well as subcentres with church, shops and public house, but the distance of these from the town centre was too great. Socially there was a clear imbalance in the age structure of the population, and there was considerable dissatisfaction at the inadequate social facilities provided in the early years.

HATFIELD (Hertfordshire), though designated as a new town, was really an expanded town on a site of 2,380 acres with a planned population of 25,000, and was intended to house workers in existing industries. It consisted of seven neighbourhoods, almost exclusively two-storey development. Here a youth centre was established from the start, run jointly by the Development Corporation and the De Havilland Aircraft Company in an old house provided by the latter. This centre was used for welcoming new residents and for old people's clubs, and at least one teenage member of every family was a member of the centre. A second centre was built by voluntary labour.

CRAWLEY (Sussex) was designated with an area of 6,047 acres. The population of 9,500 in the original village was to be expanded to 50,000 with an allowance for growth to 70,000 by 1981. Nine neighbourhoods were created, each with a primary school and again mostly of two-storey houses. There was insufficient mixing of house types, and the social amenities originally provided were inadequate, resulting in much the same problems that had afflicted Stevenage.

HEMEL HEMPSTEAD (Hertfordshire) was also an expanded town rather than a new town, with an area of 5,910 acres and a growth from the original population of 21,000 to a planned population of 60,000. It consisted of six neighbourhoods, mainly of two-storey houses. It suffered less than a new town from insufficient social amenities.

HARLOW (Essex) was planned around an existing village of 4,500 on an area of 6,320 acres with a planned population of 60,000, later increased to 80,000. There were fourteen neighbourhoods with 20 per cent of the housing in the form of flats. It also suffered from a slow provision of social amenities.

NEWTON AYCLIFFE (Co. Durham), one of the new towns outside the London region, was planned on 867 acres for a population of 10,000, later increased to 20,000. Its size was not adequate to support all the necessary social amenities and it was considered that the density of development was too low.

EAST KILBRIDE (Lanarkshire), one of two Scottish new towns, was planned on an area of 10,500 acres, of which 2,500 were for the town, the rest for a green belt, with a population of 50,000, increased later to 70,000. It was planned in four neighbourhoods, 36 per cent of the housing consisting of three- and four-storey flats. Social amenities lagged behind housing development.

PETERLEE (East Durham) was planned with a population of 30,000 on 2,350 acres in residential areas of between 5,000 and 7,500, each divided into two or three smaller units. Ten per cent of the housing was in the form of flats. There were insufficient amenities for the young until a Community Association formed by residents provided halls and common-rooms in the neighbourhood centres.

WELWYN GARDEN CITY (Hertfordshire) was an expansion of the Ebenezer Howard inspired Garden City built between the wars. From its original population of 18,500 a planned one of 50,000 was allowed for in four main areas, each served by a centre and subcentres. There was a notable separation of housing into different social groups, which perpetuated the class distinctions of the original Garden City. Despite the origins of this new town, there was the usual shortage of social amenities.

GLENROTHES (Ayrshire) had a designated area of 5,730 acres, of which 1,950 were set aside for built-up development, and a planned population of 30,000, with provision for an increase to 50,000 with higher densities to meet the overspill from Glasgow. This was to depend on new industries replacing the collieries. Originally 22 per cent of the housing was in the form of flats, but this was to be reduced eventually to 16.6 per cent. There was an active Community Association arising out of the old mining community.

BASILDON (Essex) had an original population of 25,000, made up of villages in the region, and had a planned population of 80,000, later increased to 106,000, on 7,818 acres. Housing was generally of two storeys. Basildon suffered from a particularly serious shortage of social amenities. Although designated in January 1949, by 1955 there were only three temporary community halls, all built by voluntary labour. What have since been described as 'virile social organizations' were pressing for permanent accommodation while making do with their temporary buildings, but although the situation had improved by 1961, the provision of amenities was still lagging far behind demand.

BRACKNELL (Berkshire) had a designated area of 1,860 acres and a planned population of 25,000, later increased to 3,286 acres and 54,000 people, with provision for eventual growth to 60,000. It was planned in four neighbourhoods, each with smaller units. There was a segregation of housing by social class.

CWMBRAN (Monmouthshire) had an original population of 13,000 and a planned population of 35,000 on 3,160 acres. It was to be comprised of seven neighbourhoods, each with a primary school and shopping centre. Ten per cent of the housing was in the form of flats. The social amenities were generally attached to the schools.

CORBY (Northamptonshire), with an original population of 17,000 and a designated area of 2,500 acres, had a planned population of 40,000, later increased to 55,000, with provision for natural growth to 75,000 on an increased area of 4,100 acres. Corby was a single industry town based upon Stewarts & Lloyds steelworks, and this produced social problems common to such an environment.

Certain facts emerge from this survey, the most remarkable among which, particularly in view of the recommendations of the New Towns Commission, was the failure in most cases to provide adequate social amenities. In addition, the instances of segregation of housing by social class, the example of the single industry town which cannot conceivably provide the varied interests suggested by the Commission, or even a variety of employment possibilities, and the case of Newton Aycliffe, which seemed totally inadequate in concept, all bring into question the success of the new towns. Nevertheless, success is claimed for the programme as a whole both by economists and planners of the 'garden city' school, even while they accept some of the failings. In social terms it is not easy to make a clear assessment in a period of chronic housing shortage. The same was true in the case of Dagenham. Significantly or coincidentally— who can say?—the new town built closest to Dagenham, Basildon, was the one most poorly provided for in social amenities.

In terms of the *Greater London Plan* certain doubts arise. There would appear to be a contradiction from the first if, on the one hand, it was assumed that there would be no new industry in London or the Home Counties, while on the other the new towns were to be self-sufficient in terms of employment and not become dormitories for London. New industries were established in the new towns, not all of them moved out of central London, but in time they proved to be insufficient and a considerable number of new-town dwellers commuted to London for the white-collar employment which was lacking in the new towns themselves. What was not sufficiently appreciated was the increasing proportion of white-collar workers to manual workers and only much later, when office building in London was restricted and office development in the new towns could offer decentralization, did the situation improve. In physical terms the new towns are all essentially suburban in character, and there is a monotony of building form as well as in the type of housing provided. The relatively long distances from house to centre and inadequate public transport have encouraged the use of the private car so that, with industrial areas usually on one side of the town, there can be traffic problems at peak hours. This all adds up to a situation far from ideal, and the planning of a later generation of new towns shows that these factors are not unimportant to the ultimate success or failure of the basic concept.

In 1947 came the second step in the establishment of an official planning policy in the form of the Town and Country Planning Act. The combination of this Act and the New Towns Act set the pattern not only of official planning policy, but also of the ideas and training of a new profession of town planners, for twenty years. The 1947 Act established two policies: on the one hand, local authorities, with whom executive power was vested, were required to prepare and submit to the Ministry of Town and Country Planning (later the Ministry of Housing), development plans for their area showing the proposed land use and general lines of future development; on the other hand, these same authorities were required to regulate all forms of new building development. The combination of positive and negative action has produced a sort of split personality in the planning profession, half of whom were concerned with producing development plans, the other half with controlling and restricting development. The Act was based upon land use rather than social activities. It sought to establish a pattern of land use by zoning, based upon the traditional or predominant use of land in a particular area. Once the zones of use were established, and they were generally mutually exclusive, it became virtually impossible to build or develop for another use or purpose in that zone. Coloured 'town maps' were prepared showing the different zones in prescribed colour, the 'white land' being green belt or agricultural land on which no development of any kind would be permitted.

Thus an extremely rigid framework was laid down which did not take into account the possible social benefits of diverse activities, taking place in a given area, or the possible social and economic changes that might be expected to take place in a society which was not static. The importance of land use from the point of view of strategic planning had been demonstrated by Dudley Stamp, who had carried out a mammoth land-use survey of England and Wales. But the adoption of land use as the controlling tool of planning policy was a mechanistic approach to a basically human problem, and as such was inherently at variance with the professed aims of the Welfare State.

This mechanistic approach was further emphasized by the negative side of the Act, which sought to regulate building development not only in terms of zones of use but also in terms of the permitted densities of development for the particular uses, and even in terms of the appearance of the buildings. The whole emphasis was on conformity. Zoned-use areas conformed to the traditional or predominant uses of the areas at the time; densities conformed to the existing ranges of density; the buildings were to be in keeping with the general appearance of existing development. By means of the

density and use regulations, high-density commercial development was confirmed as the appropriate building form for city
centres, and low-density residential development for the suburbs.
In other words the existing pattern, however unsatisfactory it may
have been, and for whatever reasons—good or bad—it had evolved,
was formally and officially established as the one to which everyone
concerned was legally required to conform. As regards appearance,
there arose a system of censorship of design by local planning committees, composed of groups of councillors with no specialist knowledge or appreciation of architectural values, who acted rather like
the Watch Committees to preserve existing standards of taste, however good or bad. Unlike the Watch Committees, these local planning committees did not always have professional advisers with the
skill or knowledge to advise them sensibly. At the time the Act came
into force, the profession of town planning was in its infancy, and
there were very few qualified men. Local authorities only rarely
had qualified architects in senior positions. Usually the official
planning officer was the borough engineer or the borough surveyor,
who might be highly qualified in his technical capacity, but totally
unqualified in terms of planning or architectural matters.

I have emphasized the negative qualities of the Planning Act
because it is now clear to most planners and architects that the
basis upon which it operated is not the best one to achieve the
necessary comprehensive planning which takes into account all the
relevant social, economic and physical factors. At the same time,
without the Act and its subsequent amending acts, the development
which took place after the war would have been totally chaotic and
might well have had far worse consequences. Moreover, it has
encouraged the growth of a planning profession which has studied
the problems and enabled us to see how a more effective system
might be developed. It also established official responsibility : in
other words, it killed the nineteenth-century *laissez-faire* attitude
of government to the problems of town and country development
once and for all, with all the social implications that follow. It
established machinery by which planning policies might operate
and an acceptance of them by society as a whole.

It is interesting to compare this situation with that in the United
States. As recently as 1962, Raymond Vernon, an economist who

lter Gropius
Corbusier

Frank Lloyd Wright
Ludwig Mies van der Rohe

1950s speculative housing: Ham Common, Surrey, by Eric Lyons for Span Developments.
1960s builders' speculative housing: Richmond, Surrey.

dustrialized housing at Livingston, Scotland.
bitat, Montreal, by Moshe Safdie: model of the scheme.

Industrialized housing in Eastern Europe.

directed the New York Metropolitan Region Study, advocated an effective system of land-use planning in order to overcome some of the defects of the existing zoning ordinances which, he claimed, were largely ineffective in urban areas. He wrote: 'The kind of land-use planning that is needed for the major urban areas of America is planning which takes cognizance of the total land-use needs of the area. The localities will have to turn in their weapons of war to some authority whose mandate is broader than their own and will have to be prepared to accept the decisions which issue from that higher level.'[1]

Vernon's thesis described the deterioration of urban areas during and since the nineteenth century in America along lines broadly similar to what we have seen in Britain during the same period. The difference between the two situations is the much larger area of land available for development around most American cities, and the accepted use of the private car, making the development of low-density suburban areas on a vast scale feasible. The typical plot of land for a middle-class American family house is often half an acre, and, as Vernon says, 'the overwhelming bulk of new housing in the post-war period was ranch-house-in-the-suburb'. The average density of family house development in rural or upper-middle-class areas in England is eight houses to the acre. Suburban development usually lies nearer twelve to the acre (i.e. fifty persons to the acre).

The stratification of income groups in housing 'belts' around the cities of America is more clearly marked than in Britain, and the tendency of small local authorities to use zoning ordinances to preserve the standards or 'class' of their newer and richer residential neighbourhoods while permitting changes of use in run-down and therefore poorer neighbourhoods, was one of the factors that prompted Vernon's plea for land-use planning at a higher level. Nevertheless, his thesis still basically accepts some stratification, with the poorer classes living in the older suburban belts, the buildings suitably rehabilitated, the very rich living in city centres, and the great middle classes in the suburbs. Unless, of course, the middle classes are prepared to be interested enough in large redeveloped

---

[1] Raymond Vernon, *The Myth and Reality of Our Urban Problems* (Cambridge, Mass.: Harvard University Press, 1962).

C

central city areas to make their development commercially viable.

We can now, perhaps, appreciate rather more that the Planning Act of 1947 and the acceptance of central and local government financial responsibilities in the field of planning, housing and comprehensive redevelopment, give us opportunities which have been sadly lacking in the United States.

I have discussed briefly the new towns designated between 1946 and 1951 and have looked at some of their failings. At the same time there was a considerable volume of redevelopment in the bombed cities of Britain, and new building programmes emerged from the new social welfare programmes, notably the school building programme. In London the work of rebuilding was divided largely between the LCC and the local boroughs, with planning control in the hands of the LCC. Larger housing developments were firmly on the neighbourhood pattern established by the *County of London Plan* and in the new towns. An example was the Lansbury Estate in Poplar which was included in the 1951 Festival of Britain as a 'live' exhibit of architecture and planning. Stepney and Poplar had been allocated eleven neighbourhood units as part of the plan and Lansbury was one of the first to be completed. It was predominantly low-rise building, with the bulk of the housing in the form of two-storey terraces, but with flats of three storeys. Its conception could be said to be that of an urban village, but in the context of the East End of London, and with its population working not only in the local docks but more and more in the City and West End, it was inconceivable that it should remain socially a village or neighbourhood in any exclusive sense. And this may well be the core of the problem in the neighbourhood idea.

Many writers have referred to London as a collection of villages. In the sense that it swallowed up villages in the course of spreading into the surrounding countryside, and that the centres of those villages often remained as the 'subcentres' of suburban London, like Hampstead, Highgate, Harrow-on-the-Hill in the north or Camberwell, Dulwich, Putney in the south, this is true. But it is a superficial assessment. From the time the villages were overrun the population of the area was dependent on London as a whole for its livelihood, and as often as not travelled daily to and from the central area to work. Friends and relatives might live in many other parts of the city. Local shopping and entertainment on an everyday basis were always supplemented by large-item or specialized shopping and periodic special entertainment in the centre. This was of the essence of city life. After the 1939-45 war the trend towards mobility, exemplified by the family car, and the slackening in importance of the local entertainment facilities in the face of television, have accentuated the loosening of local ties on the neighbourhood scale. Perhaps these trends were not so clear in 1945, but the basic dependence of the locality on the whole city was a fact. The neighbourhood concept was at least partially an idealized concept of what the city should be, and that concept was the garden city, with its innate fear of the urban city.

Later housing schemes in London tended to abandon the idea of the neighbourhood, while still retaining local social facilities. Churchill Gardens, Pimlico, is a good example. A competition organized by the City of Westminster was won by two young architects and developed over a period from 1948 to 1960. It is a high-density scheme, mainly of flats in blocks of eight storeys with lower blocks of maisonettes on four floors. It is planned around a number of interlinked courtyards and includes shops, library, community centre, nursery school and play-spaces. Socially it was planned to include a range of income groups from professional to unskilled workers. Probably as a result of the interest and preparedness of the middle-class professionals to involve themselves in local affairs as community leaders, a vigorous community association has been established and flourishes, running the community centre, with groups for young and old people, and a wide range of activities. But this is certainly no village concept. It is a most urban development with much of the life and vigour which the varied population of an urban community can provide, and a background of buildings that have weathered well and provide an environment with its own identity, but not overpowering in any way.

The LCC Architects' Department, which was effectively established in 1949 when the housing architects were brought into a new department and away from the Valuers' Department where they had existed hitherto, attracted many younger architects under the leadership of Robert Matthew, and new ideas began to develop in the form of new buildings. The landmark of this period was the estate at Roehampton, built in the late 'fifties. This scheme was to a large extent a reaction against the low-density housing which had prevailed in the new towns and around many of the cities, and was much influenced by the ideas of Corbusier and the Radiant City, both in planning and in the form of the buildings. On a very beautiful site overlooking Richmond Park, a hillside with a variety of large trees, the housing was planned in a series of tall slab blocks of maisonettes, point blocks of flats, with four-storey blocks lining the main access roads, and groups of single-storey old people's houses in clusters, combining with schools and community buildings to provide areas of low building. The open spaces consisted of undulating expanses of grass, creating a parkland atmosphere.

This was a new concept of suburbia. It was not urban in the sense that Pimlico was. It was on the south-west edge of London, and built at a much lower density. In fact it was closest in atmosphere to the developments that were taking place in and around Stockholm, where new towns were being planned largely on the basis of blocks of flats rather than small houses.

We have no survey to show how successful Roehampton has been in social terms, but it was planned with reasonably adequate social facilities, and certainly gives the impression of being an eminently pleasant place to live in. Even so it had its shortcomings. The increase in car ownership that took place in the decade after its construction was not foreseen by the planners, and little provision was made for parking. Consequently all the roads on the estate are now lined with parked cars, which in the parkland environment is visually even more disruptive than it is elsewhere. Since the parkland is also free play-space and there is no segregation of cars from pedestrians, the cars present a hazard to young children. Architecturally the contrast between the four-storey blocks, which are of brick construction, and the tall blocks, which are built of concrete, is visually disturbing.

One of the most interesting housing schemes to evolve anywhere during the 1950s was the Park Hill development in Sheffield. The two phases of this scheme provided 2,387 dwellings on land originally occupied by 1,040 slum-houses. The buildings are planned on steeply sloping land near the centre of town, overlooking the valley in which the main railway line and central station are situated. Basically each of the two phases is a single tall building meandering over the site and forming irregular semi-enclosed spaces at ground level. The roof level of the buildings remains constant, so that the height of the buildings varies, and use is made of the slope to link the ground levels with pedestrian streets in the buildings. Access from the streets to floors above and below by means of stairs within the flats and maisonettes enables the number of levels of access to be reduced from the normal access gallery on every floor, or every alternate floor, and thereby makes it economical to increase the depth of the gallery so that it really forms a street, along which electric delivery vehicles can run. Schools, play-spaces, shops and pubs are planned on the ground floor and independently in the open spaces.

This scheme represents high-density urban housing on a large scale and in a form which could conceivably develop into a complete city centre. It could be expanded to include offices, hotels, large stores and all the other paraphernalia of the city, and become a compact and human environment. At the time it was built there were other interesting developments in Sheffield, including a multi-storey shopping centre and market, but on the opposite side of the railway from Park Hill.

While these were not the only schemes of importance or interest built in the two decades after the war, they do represent the high points of thought and imagination in an otherwise dull mass of housing. Two-storey houses in one form or another formed the bulk of the new housing built by local authorities and private developers. The types and form of these houses related closely to the speculative housing built in the 1930s, with minor refinements. The visually disruptive semi-detached house remained a perennial favourite, and in 1950 even the most progressive architectural schools set exercises for its design.

The terrace house was also much in evidence, but was more popular with local authorities than private developers, so that there was a sort of class distinction in operation, terrace houses being synonymous with 'council housing' for the working class and semi-detached with the middle-class, privately built house. The experiments with prefabricated building made in the late 'forties and early 'fifties, to find ways of building permanently with non-traditional materials, since there was a shortage of traditional kinds, reflected the popular taste. This taste was reinforced by the local planning committees, as I have suggested earlier. So, on the whole, nothing very new came out of the two-storey housing until the late 'fifties.

With flats there was more thought and imagination. There had to be, since there had been so little done in this field in the past. Of flats built between the wars by local authorities and private developers it was still true to say that in Britain we did not understand how to design them, in comparison with other countries. The main source of influence after the war was Scandinavia, but this was more superficial than positive. The basic planning was more closely related to the tenements of the nineteenth-century charities, particularly in relation to the form of access. The open gallery access was favoured on grounds of economy, despite its many disadvantages, which included lack of privacy and exposure to weather. But regulations made it impossible at that time to build internal and artificially ventilated bathrooms, and this was a considerable restriction in planning. A comparison between English and Danish plans of the same period shows basically higher space standards in England, but poorer planning and equipment, and more wasteful use of space. This is still true today.

At the same time there was a growing consciousness about the problems of housing standards, both in planning and construction. In 1944 the Ministry of Health and Ministry of Works issued the first *Housing Manual*, which prescribed minimum standards for different types of housing, as well as making many non-mandatory recommendations. The Housing Act of 1935 had established certain standards regarding bedroom sizes and based the number of persons to be accommodated on the number of bedrooms in a house. This set the basis for housing densities under the Town and Country Planning Acts. The *Housing Manual* went much further than previous codes and was itself revised in 1949, and supplemented every two years thereafter until the Report of the Central Housing Advisory Committee (better known as the Parker Morris

Report) in 1961.[2] The Ministry of Works published a series of *Post-War Building Studies* which looked at various planning and technical aspects of building and made recommendations which, though not mandatory, were widely accepted and incorporated into normal practice. These included codes of daylighting. In general, much research began on planning and technical problems, and the results were incorporated little by little as the work developed. The groundwork proved invaluable to the more sophisticated research and development work later undertaken by the Ministries of Housing, Public Building and Works, Health and Education, and by university departments, the Building Research Station, and numerous industry based organizations.

[2] Ministry of Housing and Local Government, *Homes for Today and Tomorrow* (London: HMSO, 1961), Report of the Sub-Committee under the chairmanship of Sir Parker Morris, appointed by the Central Housing Committee 'to consider the standards of design and equipment applicable to family dwellings and other forms of residential accommodation, whether provided by public authorities or by private enterprise, and to make recommendations'.

Chapter 4

The Mass Building Programmes

The significant factor of the post-1945 period, not only in Britain but in all European countries, was the acceptance by the State of responsibilities for financing, building and subsidizing housing, mainly for those too poor to be able to buy or rent accommodation at current market levels. The basic reason for this was a general post-war state of acute housing shortage and need. In industrially advanced countries like Britain and those of Western Europe, there had been a shortage before the war. In all countries, and particularly those of Eastern Europe, the devastation of urban areas during the war created a situation of intense gravity. Reconstruction of devastated cities was one of the first priorities once communications had been established and the distribution of food reorganized. In terms of devastation the countries worst affected were the Soviet Union, Poland and Germany. But overall and whatever political party or régime held power, the responsibility of the State actively to participate in the housing of its people was accepted and established. Similarly the expectation of a sudden increase in the birth-rate after the war forced governments to enter into large-scale school building programmes to cope with what became known as the 'post-war bulge' in the population of schoolchildren. In fact the whole climate of the immediate post-war years reflected a general desire for social justice and the construction of a better world. Any architectural student starting his studies within five years after the war was encouraged to believe that he held this great reconstruction with all its social implications in the palm of his hand.

The realities of the situation were far from ideal. Industry had either been destroyed, as in Germany, or totally geared to war production. Building materials and components were therefore in short supply, and one form or another of building restriction applied in most countries, first to ensure that essential building had priority, and second that available materials were used to their best advantage. In Britain bricks were available but timber was in very short supply, having to be imported from countries like the Soviet Union, which had urgent needs itself, or bought in a market where world demand was at a peak. As a result of the shortages of traditional materials on the one hand, and the urgency of needs on the other, there were a number of experiments aimed at producing houses by non-traditional methods, and as quickly as possible.

The result was the 'prefab' house, generally constructed of steel and asbestos cement and erected in large estates on any available open space including bombed sites, in and around the urban areas. At least one of the designs, the 'Arcon' house, was of an extremely high standard of design and technique, and there are a few still in use even though they were designed for a maximum life of ten years. Unfortunately this idea of its temporary nature became so much a part of the popular conception of prefabrication (or industrialization, as it is now called), that many years passed before it became widely accepted in Britain in the field of housing. Perhaps it was natural that after six years of extreme insecurity, following upon an even longer period of economic insecurity for most people, the demand should be psychologically for permanent houses, built in traditional styles. In those countries where industry had been destroyed there was labour available, so that the traditional on-site labour based methods were anyway the only ones practicable for reconstruction. Only after industry re-established itself on a peacetime basis and life returned to normal was there much scope for radically new ideas in building.

This reliance on traditional methods, though unavoidable, was perhaps unfortunate, since the problems were of such a scale that they demanded a new all-round approach. One of the criticisms often levelled at modern architecture is that, in fields like housing, it is monotonous and dull compared with the building of the past. Yet as we have seen earlier, the vast mass of nineteenth-century housing was unutterably dull and monotonous, and in effect, after 1945, we were simply building more or less in the same way and with materials similar to those used in nineteenth-century houses. The attempts to be 'modern' were usually in the form of larger windows, which often were out of proportion to the size of the house, and other 'micro' variations on the old theme. The standards of architectural and social awareness evident in the design of housing in the years immediately after the war were clearly inadequate. Essentially it was impossible for the planners and architects who were engaged in the programme of housing to think on a large enough scale.

As was pointed out in the previous chapter, town planning only became a fully and officially accepted profession after the New Towns Act of 1946 in Britain, and architects were only employed on a large scale in government-subsidized housing after 1945. The professional men were therefore in short supply, and those who were available had limited experience of the problems. It is not surprising that the results should have proved inadequate both in scale and quality. The pressures in different countries also affected their attitudes to the problem. In those countries most devastated by the war the problem was of building in quantity at speed: quality of design was necessarily of secondary importance. This immediate problem was not so acute in Britain. On the other hand, just as the machinery of industry was overstrained if not actually worn out as a result of war production and the lack of replacement, so the general stock of housing had suffered from six years of relative neglect and lack of replacement, and in any case was largely obsolete and run down even before the war. Because the situation was less acute, the volume of new housing built in Britain did not compare with West Germany or the Soviet Union, where immediate rebuilding was essential. The pressures in those two countries, inducing as they did greater experience of rebuilding within a short period, may well have contributed to higher standards in the long run than those in Britain. However that may be, the fact is that in Britain, in the immediate post-war years, we planned more carefully than ever before, but built houses of a technical and aesthetic standard roughly equivalent to those of the pre-war period.

It takes five years full-time study to complete an architectural course. Perhaps, therefore, it is significant that a sort of turning-point was reached in Britain with the Festival of 1951. By then the first generation of architects who had been trained entirely after the war were at work. Most of them had not been deeply involved in the Festival itself; that was the work of the pre-war generation of architects. The post-1951 movement was in a new direction, much more 'solid' and even serious than the gay frivolities of the South Bank. The exhibition itself displayed signs of all the influences that had been at work on a generation of architects and designers growing up in an age of 'utility' furniture and clothing, severe restrictions on materials and building costs, a period generally grey in atmosphere, in which the defeat of Nazism was already overshadowed by the Atom Bomb and the Cold War, and in which food rationing had become more severe for a period than during the war itself.

It represented, for those designers taking part, the first real opportunity to show off, and show off they did, though by no means in any vulgar way. Indeed, one of the significant things about the South Bank Exhibition was its good taste, its gentle frivolity, its chichi (a popular phrase in the early 'fifties). Its gaiety was Brighton rather than Blackpool. Yet in many ways it was a dead end. The Festival style lingered on in furniture and other household items, and its lettering styles can still be seen in provincial shopping centres, but from the architectural point of view it went nowhere. It claimed to herald the arrival of modern architecture. Certainly one building on the South Bank, the Royal Festival Hall, had individual distinction, and its balconied interior and, until recently, fussy elevations, were a permanent landmark of the Festival. Despite its shortcomings, its foyers demonstrate how modern architecture can create a lively and festive series of spaces for large numbers of people.

However important the Festival Hall itself may be, the 'live' architectural exhibition which formed part of the Festival merely revealed the architectural deficiencies of so-called modern housing. The site, one of the neighbourhoods in Poplar which had been outlined in the *County of London Plan*, was called the Lansbury Estate. It is, perhaps, not too harsh to call it a working man's Hampstead Garden Suburb, because in planning terms that was how it was conceived. One of its two churches was neo-classical, the other vaguely Scandinavian. The houses followed what I have already described as the general post-war pattern : refined 1930s style.

Against this background and from a new generation of architects growing up professionally in the Welfare State there came a profound reaction which has slowly filtered through the attitudes current in the 'fifties and began, during the late 'sixties, to produce a new approach to the building of houses. To see where this started we must look back to the 1930s and even beyond, to Corbusier and his Unité d'habitation, his vertical neighbourhood. The potentialities of high-density housing, not just tall blocks of flats, but a variety of dwelling types together with certain community facilities and services on the lines Corbusier had suggested so long ago, and which he was at last able to build in Marseilles in the 1950s, were among the ideas which occupied the minds of architectural students at that time. Another was the potential of prefabrication, in relation to housing. A third was the possibility of a marriage of these two ideas and the mixing of high and low buildings in the context of the new town situation. Contemporary students were sensitive to the architectural failings of the new towns and were concerned about their social failings as well. There was much talk of balanced communities and how architects and planners could help to achieve them. So it was that in the 'fifties a number of the most able young architects joined the LCC Architects' Department, where they formulated standards in housing that excelled most previous work and even that of private developers for a relatively high income group, standards that others were forced to follow.

There were precedents. In particular, two housing competitions had been held for London sites, and from the many entries two successful schemes emanated. The first of these, described in the previous chapter, was Churchill Gardens in Pimlico, designed by Powell and Moya and built by Westminster Council. The other was the Golden Lane housing scheme in the City of London, which, though not as successful in many ways as Pimlico, led to the complete redevelopment of the Barbican by the architects who had won the original competition, Chamberlin Powell and Bon.

The culmination of the work of the LCC architects in housing of this period was the Roehampton Estate, also described in the previous chapter. The Sheffield Park Hill scheme was also of this period, so one can see quite clearly a strong move away from the rather indeterminate architecture of the immediate post-war years in housing.

Of developments in the 'sixties I shall speak later, because during the period from the late 'forties onwards there were highly significant developments going on in the field of educational buildings which produced a sort of feed-back in housing during the 'sixties. The post-war bulge of schoolchildren was the incentive for a programme of school building and of studies by the Ministry of Education into the rationalization of the programme. The programme was under-taken by individual education authorities, and the authority which pioneered a new approach to the problem was Hertfordshire County Council. They adopted a policy of rationalization of their building programme by designing what was then called a prefabricated system of construction and components, and what would now be called an industrialized system; a kind of construction set of standardized parts designed for the particular programme of school building and allowing assembly in a variety of ways on different sites. This naturally involved dimensional co-ordination which, in its turn, involved a detailed study of the functional and spatial needs in order to determine acceptable dimensions for the parts. This may appear superficially to be a fairly simple and obvious step to take. In fact it involves all sorts of problems if one is to achieve not only a sufficient degree of standardization of the parts to make for cheap production and easy erection, but also for flexi-bility of use.

The prefabricated houses built immediately after the war were completely designed units, self-contained and not requiring varia-tions in plan, shape or arrangement on site. A school is a very different problem. There is a story about an American specialist engineer who had worked for many years on the problems of pre-fabrication and dimensional co-ordination. It is said that during the war he was asked by a government department, which was engaged in building military installations all over the country, to set up a team with unlimited financial resources and to spend a year of study to find the ideal three-dimensional planning module to allow for the maximum flexibility in use and for application to any type of building. At the end of a year he reported to the government with an impressive collection of documents, all of which proved conclusively that the ideal module was 9" x 4½" x 3" —the dimensions of a brick. Obviously there is no such thing as an ideal module in the abstract. One has to find a series of inter-related dimensions which will work on an additive basis for the building, to provide a series of components which fit in reasonably with the planning requirements.

From the earliest Hertfordshire schools up to the more sophisticated industrialized systems in present use, a planning grid has been established on the basis of a given dimension for a basic module. For traditional buildings built in brick, the brick dimension was in fact used as a module for the external walls at least. What the pre-fab or industrialized system does is to use a basic module in three dimensions and throughout the building. Essentially this is nothing new. From the moment in time when man first began to use a measuring-rod and to establish certain values to measure distance we have been using modules. Measurement sprang from man's relating himself to the environment by measuring with his hand, his fingers, his arms. What we call dimensional co-ordination or modular design is only a further step in the process of formalizing and selecting certain convenient units of measurement for a particular use. The problem is that of selection of the most convenient units. One has to balance the requirements of room dimensions, door openings and so on against the most commonly manufactured sizes of basic building materials. In the long run the two should be co-ordinated so that the manufactured sizes relate to the modular dimensions in such a way as to reduce wastage of material by trimming and cutting. This was what was undertaken by the Hertfordshire County Architects' Department and it produced good schools speedily and as cheaply as if they were built by traditional methods. The system was further developed by the Ministry of Education, which set up a research and development group of architects and other specialists, and a number of schools were built under the guidance of the Ministry in different parts of the country, by means of it.

The experience gained in these early years showed fairly clearly that the economy of industrialized systems, particularly as they became more sophisticated, depended on there being a large enough production run of components to make them competitive. The scope of one education authority, particularly among those operating in largely rural areas, was limited to the number of schools that could be programmed over a reasonable period. The answer seemed to be that groups of local authorities should pool their programmes and design teams into consortiums, to achieve longer production runs and co-ordination in design over a wider area. As a result of this, CLASP[1] was established and, among other consortiums, SCOLA.[2]

The work of CLASP received international notice from its participation in the Milan Triennale of 1961, when the system was used to construct the British Pavilion. The Italian Ministry of Education is now using the CLASP system, suitably modified. CLASP has also demonstrated that it is adaptable to building schemes other than those for schools. It has been used for a wide range of public buildings and for universities. It is a proven success for what one writer has called 'co-operation between managerially revolutionized builders and deprofessionalized architects'.[3]

What is interesting about the school building systems is that they have created a new aesthetic in school design. They lent themselves well to new educational ideas, particularly in primary schools, and have enabled these new schools to be much more informal, light and friendly places, less institutional and much more in scale with the children, than earlier buildings. The same could have been achieved by traditional means, but the fact that this more informal pattern has been established means that it would be difficult, if not impossible, to get an imposing, formalistic school built at all, and this is surely a step in the right direction.

Yet at the same time one cannot claim that this is the complete solution. Aesthetically, many problems remain unresolved within the systems at present in use and many of the best architects work-

[1] The participants in CLASP (Consortium of Local Authorities Special Programme) were: the Department of Education and Science, the Ministry of Public Buildings and Works, the Scottish Development Department; the County Councils of Derbyshire, Durham, Glamorgan, Lanarkshire, Nottinghamshire, Staffordshire, Warwickshire and West Riding; the County Boroughs of Coventry, Gateshead, Leicester and Manchester; together with universities and other associate members.

[2] SCOLA (Second Consortium of Local Authorities) was made up of: the Department of Education and Science; the County Councils of Cheshire, Dorset, Gloucestershire, Hampshire, Leicestershire, Northumberland, Shropshire, West Sussex and Worcestershire; the County Boroughs of Leeds and Sheffield; and various associate members.

[3] Stanley Alderson, *Britain in the Sixties: Housing* (Harmondsworth, Middx: Penguin Books, 1962).

ing today would hesitate before using them. Apparent are a certain monotony of rhythm and thinness of form, which are often disguised by tile-hanging and other inappropriate means. There is a lack of the drama which the best modern building can produce and often a tendency towards a rather amorphous overall character. Junctions between blocks of different height and form seem to be difficult to handle and a lot of ugly and even crude detailing is evident. There is room for development and certainly the schools of the future should show a considerable advance on those already built.

Curiously a similar approach has not been used in the field of university building, besides one or two exceptional instances like York. The development and extension of the universities followed in step upon the development first of primary then secondary schools, coping with the post-war bulge. But whereas the schools programmes were tackled with a good deal of rationalization and co-ordination, the universities have been planned individually and with no clear pattern. Perhaps it is the lingering image of the university in terms of Oxbridge that somehow encourages people to create the new universities in this rather monastic and dignified style. Perhaps, even more, it is a certain subconscious inferiority complex in relation to Oxford and Cambridge that is responsible for this tendency to status building in the newer universities. Whatever the cause, they differ widely from each other in many aspects, and particularly in their basic organization, whether on a collegiate basis or not, but they are virtually similar in their attempt to create not only an individual image, which is understandable, but also a sense of the monumental, a self-assertion that is not altogether appropriate in our time. They reveal an attempt to set apart that whole section of the educational process, so far as its architectural significance is concerned, from the primary and secondary stages that precede it and from the parallel institutions of further education which are being developed alongside it, which smacks of class-consciousness. I am not suggesting that universities should look like schools, but that, if rationalization and standardization could produce a successful and flexible range of school buildings, could not the same approach have been used for educational buildings as a whole?

Undoubtedly many of the new university buildings rank among

the best examples of contemporary architecture; the overall standard of design is extremely high, in comparison with other fields of building. But with so many of them set in isolation from the urban centres which they serve, in beautiful tracts of parkland or open country, the problem of design is of a different order, and the temptation to create an individual monument very great. The number of people going to universities is increasing vastly. One of the aspects of the new institutions that is disturbing and which is part and parcel of this 'apartheid' approach, is the building of large campuses of student hostels and halls of residence. Surely it is time that we thought of housing for students as part of the overall housing problem. Surely by planning accommodation for students in the community alongside everyone else, we could help to break down some of the many and complex barriers involving class, generation gaps and so on between the community and students.

Clearly these are grounds for discussion with educationalists, sociologists and government agencies, and since architects and planners are deeply concerned with the image of the university, they have a particular responsibility to raise these questions. There is also quite clearly a general movement among students and many of the younger teachers to reappraise the role and status of the university in society. The line of thought is away from rigid, formalized, imposing institutions towards ones essentially democratic in concept and in their relation to society as a whole. The intellectual power-house concept is surely dying, and if this is so, then the buildings we have been constructing for our universities will be obsolete in a few years time.

So far we have looked at two broad aspects of the mass building programmes instituted or subsidized by the State. During the period we are considering, there was at least as much building carried on in Britain by private developers, and during the 'fifties there was the now famous, or infamous, property boom. The effect of this on the face of our urban areas and on the whole field of environmental development, the building industry and the national economy, has been considerable. The property boom was effectively created by the removal of controls on building which had been imposed after the war, and in particular by the abolition of the development charge by the 1953 Town and Country Planning Act. This produced a great boom in land values, added to by subsequent acts which provided for compensation to be paid to landowners for loss suffered from planning restrictions.

The development charge was introduced in the 1947 Town and Country Planning Act and meant in effect that all development rights in land were nationalized. The defect of this provision was that it only took account of the development value of land, not of the increase in value of land already developed. The development charge was 100 per cent of the increase in value of land for which planning permission had been granted. The result was a collapse in the land market. This might have changed if the provisions of the Act had been merely modified; by their abolition a boom situation was created overnight.

The land most affected was that which had been zoned for commercial use or which had commercial possibilities, but residential land in reasonably good suburban areas was also snapped up by the property developers. This started the great era of office building in most of the large cities, with new property companies mushrooming and deals in land bringing huge profits to the fortunate few, often without any building actually taking place. The mere granting of 'outline planning permission' for a piece of land was a guarantee of enormous capital gain for the landowner.[4] On the one hand, city centres and the best residential land were swallowed up by commercial buildings, while on the other hand less immediately profitable land increased in value through successive changes of ownership without being developed. The latter often consisted of residential areas which seemed likely to improve as neighbourhoods—that is to say, parts more recently termed 'twilight areas' where old and

[4] Officially, planning permission is granted as 'outline planning permission' or 'detailed planning permission'. The former can be given on the basis of an application form accompanied simply by a small-scale plan of the land. Building cannot begin until detailed planning permission has been received, and this requires the submission of a full set of drawings showing in detail the proposed development. Hence the ease with which outline planning permission could be obtained, i.e. without any commitment to undertake the development. In 1968 the procedure was modified by a condition which requires that development must be commenced within five years from the date of outline planning permission.

run-down houses were being bought up by people seeking reasonably cheap accommodation. These were districts of obvious housing need and land values rose steeply, so that local authorities, even if granted compulsory purchase orders for redevelopment, were forced to pay relatively inflated prices for the land. Consequently the cost of housing provision rose in proportion to land prices.

The other residential areas affected were those on the periphery of the urban regions, which were needed for larger scale housing and overspill. By the mid-'sixties the cost of land for housing, in parts immediately around central London, approached 50 per cent of the cost of the buildings themselves, or approximately £2,500 per dwelling. In 1970 land compulsorily acquired for housing by the GLC was up to £3,600 in the same area. This means that the total cost of building a three-bedroom dwelling for five people in central London is nearing the £10,000 level, allowing for the cost of land, of construction, professional fees, legal charges, etc. With the level of interest-rates as high as they are now, rents will increase considerably.

The effect of the property boom on actual building costs was also considerable. During the 'fifties and early 'sixties the building industry concentrated much of its resources and effort on the commercial sector. Not only were there larger profits to be made from office building than from housing, but in order to simplify the financing of commercial developments, many of the larger building contractors were putting up the money for building in return for a share in the development profits. 'Package deals' were offered, including feasibility studies, design, construction and even financing. Inevitably, with full order books competitiveness of tendering became less keen, while at the same time the risk element attaching to participation in the commercial building boom also helped to push up costs. The concentration of effort and resources on the commercial side, together with the full order books, meant that contractors were only willing to take on housing contracts if their profit margins were reasonably high, so that the cost of housing went up. Even so, land was the dominant feature in the increased cost of housing: between 1959 and 1961 the price of houses in Britain increased by 25 per cent, while building costs increased by 11 per cent.

The effect of the escalation of commercial building on our cities in planning terms was to aggravate transport and commuting problems and upset the balance between people living and working in central urban areas. Between 1953 and 1962 there was an increase of approximately 10 per cent (116,000) in the number of people travelling into central London to work each day, while the drop in people living in central London in the same period was about 150,000. This has exacerbated road congestion and put heavy pressure on public transport facilities, to which no satisfactory answer has yet been found. The situation deteriorated so much, and was in any case so much against the national post-war policy of dispersal of population and work from the major urban centres, that the Government was forced first to exhort industry and commerce to decentralize their administration to the outer suburbs and the new towns, and then to introduce severe restrictions on further office building in London and the south-east of England generally.

The buildings themselves have done little to enhance the character and quality of our cities. Very few office buildings have achieved the architectural standards of the new universities, for example. Here, if anywhere, there is justification in the complaints about so many 'matchboxes'. The design basis for most commercial development was first the maximum utilization of the site and the so-called 'plot ratios', ratios of the site area to the area allowed to be built upon it as laid down by the Town Planning Regulations, and generally unrelated to what was already built or was being built on adjoining sites, in terms of mass and form. Second, the concern was to get the maximum amount of lettable office space out of a building. The final product satisfied the commercial requirements first and foremost and architectural quality was sacrificed to this end. The techniques and components available were developed to achieve speedy and economical construction, but the whole operation was that of producing a saleable product for a carefully worked out market. Any concessions to architectural or environmental requirements tended to be made only under pressure from a local planning authority or the Royal Fine Arts Commission where the building was so situated or of such a size that the Commission could be brought in. The concentration of new blocks of offices in certain parts of cities, creating a wilderness of concrete, steel and glass uninhabited outside working hours, has accentuated the problems of unbalanced development. Altogether the great boom has proved to be an almost unmitigated disaster for our towns and cities.

In this period of the property boom changes were taking place in the housing field. There was considerable concern that the rate of house building was not high enough to cope with the problem, which was compounded of replacement of obsolete houses on the one hand, and providing for a growing population in the major industrial areas on the other, together with the additional problems posed by increased standards of living and expectation of still higher standards. Clearly, designs used hitherto were now inadequate, and safeguards were necessary against early obsolescence.

As a consequence several things were done by the Government. In 1957 the Rent Act removed rent control on dwellings with a rateable value of £40 and over in London, and £30 and over elsewhere. It was hoped that the removal of controls which had been in force since the war would encourage landlords to improve their properties. In fact all that happened was that rents increased and the racketeers stepped into the field at the expense of the poorest groups of tenants. By 1961 general concern over the inadequacy of the Government's housing policies had reached a head. The Central Housing Advisory Committee appointed a committee which became known as the Parker Morris Committee, 'to consider the standards of design and equipment applicable to family dwellings and other forms of residential accommodation, whether provided by public authorities or private enterprise, and to make recommendations'. A National Building Agency was established as a co-ordinating and advisory body for planning and construction and has been almost exclusively concerned with housing. A Housing Act set up a sort of pilot scheme for voluntary non-profit-making housing societies and associations, which had existed for many years, but which it was hoped could be expanded into a substantial third arm in the housing field between public and private housing. In order to speed up the rate of construction it was decided to encourage the use of industrialized building systems which had been used successfully on the Continent for housing. The National Building Agency would grant licences of approval for specific proprietary systems submitted by building contractors, and local authorities would be encouraged to use them.

At the same time, the voice of a particularly vocal group, including many architects, which had been urging high-rise housing as an answer to land shortage and to counteract the suburban sprawl of much of the newer housing, both in estates and the new towns, found receptive ears in so far as the industrialized building systems on the Continent were largely designed for high-rise buildings. In fact there was an additional subsidy from the Ministry of Housing for high-rise blocks, since they were inherently more expensive to build. One may be forgiven for thinking that high-rise building became a sort of status symbol for local authorities, since so many tall blocks of flats were built regardless of the situation or site. Architects who had not been involved in the office building boom could now make their mark with twelve- to twenty-storey structures. Contractors were given a valuable bargaining weapon, since they could with reason claim that the development of any system, even one imported from abroad, and the capital investment needed, could only be justified economically by a reliable flow of work. Local authorities were therefore encouraged to enter into large contracts of the 'package deal' variety, in which the contractor was responsible for the design and construction of large schemes under the general direction of the local authority.

The layout of the buildings on the site was dictated largely by the economic deployment of mechanical plant and equipment used in construction. One of the justifications for high-rise building, namely an increase of space around the buildings for functional uses, was effectively destroyed. Such 'amenity' spaces were never designed to have any function beyond the drawing-board. Peter Self, in his book *Cities in Flood*,[5] effectively demolishes many of the premises upon which the high-rise building programme was based. The Ronan Point disaster effectively demolished the programme itself. Here was a case where a package-deal situation allowed a contractor to build with the approval of all the technical controlling authorities, using a system which was actually dangerous. It took the deaths of several people to bring everyone to their senses.

Or did it? Much of the impetus for high-rise housing had come

[5] London: Faber & Faber, 1957.

from successful schemes such as at Roehampton, Pimlico and Park Hill, Sheffield. Yet these had all been very carefully considered, planned and executed by first-class architects and in particularly suitable situations. Even so, they are by no means faultless, and we know that Roehampton, despite its idyllic setting, leaves much to be desired. Most architects of the calibre of those who worked on these schemes had strong views about low-rise sprawling developments. But most of them would have agreed that the real need was for development which was mixed in form as well as social composition. Ideally, families living on the twentieth floor with young children needed their own sheltered terraces or balconies, and play-spaces within easy call. This was the basis of Corbusier's Unité d'habitation, the major influence on architects working on high-rise schemes. But his buildings were much too expensive for the government-subsidized system, even in France, and became more or less luxury flats.

As a result, one must consider high-rise building at lower cost for families without young children. This immediately presupposes mixed development for high-density sites, with high flats for childless families or families with older children, for single people, and houses or low blocks of maisonettes for families with young children. Already during the 'fifties architects in Britain, Switzerland and elsewhere were experimenting with what became known as low-rise, high-density housing. After Ronan Point this form suddenly became almost the fashion and, as so often happens, we are now in danger of swinging from one extreme to another.

Chapter 5

Building Industrialized

In discussing the mass building programmes since 1945 I have mentioned the post-war prefabs, the school building programmes and industrialized housing up to the time of the Ronan Point failure, and have discussed briefly some of the principles involved in rationalized building techniques. The use of industrialized building has been widespread in the industrialized countries in the past decade at least and is developing apace. The full potentials have not yet been realized and the directions of development are not yet clearly defined. Until they are, we face the possibility of future failure, not so much of a physical nature, as with Ronan Point, but of a social and aesthetic kind, which in the long run could be of far greater consequence.

For some considerable time before the Ronan Point incident, there had been mounting criticism of tower blocks of flats as a housing form, particularly for families with children. It was all too evident that there was less social contact between people living above one another and meeting only in the lift than there was when they lived side by side at or near ground level. There were particular problems for families with young children, in so far as the play areas on the ground were too remote from the mother on the 12th floor, so that either the children played in the flat, which was inconvenient, or the mother was in a fairly constant state of anxiety about her child twelve floors down. Either way there was a state of nervous tension. The higher the flats were, the greater was the feeling of isolation. Tower blocks were built without regard for the effects at ground level of wind pressures and speeds. Often the effect of a tall block was to increase, even to double the wind speed around the block at ground level, so that the open space, which was supposed to be one of the assets of this form of building, was of no practical use. The common lack of vehicle-pedestrian segregation presented further hazards for children on the ground.

The Ronan Point collapse provided the opportunity for all these criticisms to be aired publicly: it was as if everyone had been waiting for some excuse before admitting that this was the wrong form of housing. The fact that Ronan Point was built within an industrialized building system, like so many other tower blocks, was not the point which caught the public imagination at all, and outside the professions and building industry few people realized the implications of this fact.

The implications are tied up with the whole basis upon which industrialized building up to that point had been founded. The reasons for adopting the industrialized systems were basically economic. The building industry has traditionally been relatively high in labour content and low in material value. It had involved the employment on site of skilled craftsmen and semi- and unskilled labour in fairly high numbers, with a strong preponderance of casual labour. Attaining a craft skill involved a long apprenticeship, and all work in the industry took place in bad physical working conditions. The industry is still the most dangerous industry, so far as accidents at work are concerned. In a period of general industrial expansion in industries which became more heavily mechanized and automated, the incentive for the unskilled worker to endure the difficult physical conditions of a building site, the lack of security of tenure of a job, and relatively low wages, faded away. He could earn at least as much, probably more, working on a production line in a factory without all the disadvantages of the building site. Similarly, a young man looking for a trade to follow, would find the training, subsequent employment and long-term prospects offered by an engineering apprenticeship, for example, much more preferable to a building trade apprenticeship. The result has been fewer skilled building workers and fewer unskilled workers, and the calibre of both has tended to decrease as the more able and intelligent workers have tended to look to the manufacturing industries for employment.

For the building contractor there are other problems. The vagaries of the weather make a constant work flow difficult to achieve on site, particularly in the early stages of construction. The co-ordination of work, which is partly 'manufactured' on site and partly the fixing of ready-manufactured items; the numerous trades involved, and problems of demarcation between them; the problems of waste of materials due to the rough conditions of a building site; all these contribute to a situation where a product is being manufactured in conditions very difficult to control. Following the larger contracts which have become common as part of the large-scale building programmes, the number of small and medium-sized building firms has tended to decrease and most of the major building projects are carried out by contractors established on at least a regional if not a national basis. The application of rationalized business management to these companies has also tended to make them turn towards a situation which can be controlled on a more rational business basis, and, as a result, where they cannot themselves manufacture the various components, they sub-contract to specialist firms which supply and install their components. They work, therefore, with a minimum of site labour, and their job is more and more the co-ordination of specialists.

By its nature, this also leads to problems, for it only requires one sub-contractor to fall behind in his programme to put the whole operation out of gear. There is therefore every reason for the larger contracting firms to try to move as close as they can to the relatively tightly controlled situation of other manufacturing industries. This means not only taking as much building off the site as possible and into the factory, but in order to make the installation of mechanized plant and other capital equipment economically feasible, the maximum standardization of components becomes necessary to avoid constant retooling, and to enable sufficient runs of each component. This in turn reflects upon the design of the building and its components.

The tendency among architects, as a profession, has been to find ways to express their individuality of design, and in doing so they are constantly seeking new solutions to common problems, both in terms of overall planning and design, and in the methods of construction, detail and finishing. In so far as this involves a constant reappraisal of their work and development of ideas, it also means a constant improvement in standards. Nevertheless, in terms of large-scale building programmes in a social situation where there is a need for urgency and economy, it may be argued that the individual approach to this constant development is a luxury that society cannot afford. Certainly the builders have long argued that it is a luxury they cannot afford. As a result they have argued for the so-called 'package deal', in which they design and construct a building project, employing architects and other professionals within their own organizations, whom they can better control.

The use of industrialized building systems, developed as proprietary systems by the contractors, enabled them to take the whole process one rational stage further. The official encouragement of industrialized systems in the mid-'sixties by a government seeking to step up its housing programme, which was suffering as a result of the commercial property boom, gave the builders a golden opportunity which they were quick to take. This was the situation in Britain, but the basis and principles were the same elsewhere.

In the USSR the housing shortage after 1945 was critical to an extent difficult for us to imagine. During the following years an enormous effort was put into the development of systems to increase the speed of building. Dwelling plans and forms were standardized to a considerable degree and layouts and construction planned for the maximum use of large precast concrete units. The effect of using mechanized equipment was to regulate the housing layouts in a rather regimental fashion, and the resultant environmental quality was low. Nevertheless, their concentration on building in quantity has meant that today Soviet families are generally housed in postwar dwellings of a fairly even standard, but all with proper bathrooms, kitchens and amenities. A recent survey has suggested that the overall situation in the USSR is probably better than in the United States.

In France, the control exercised by architects over building contractors has never been as close as in Britain, and French contractors have tended to take much more responsibility for the detailed design of the construction and finish of buildings, particularly in the housing field. It is not surprising, therefore, that a number of the most advanced industrialized systems using precast concrete should have originated in France. It is also not surprising that, given greater freedom from architectural control, the standard of housing layouts in France should be based more on the economic use of the plant associated with the systems than on good design. Even in Denmark, where the overall standard of traditional design and layout is as good as anywhere in the world, a number of technically advanced systems have been developed, the use of which has involved the most rigid and even inhuman layout of buildings. Both French and Danish systems have been used in Britain, and the system used for Ronan Point was a modified Danish system.

Industrialized techniques have been used, therefore, for reasons of speed and economics, both in commercial situations in the capitalist countries and in urgent social situations in the USSR. But it is clear that they have introduced very real disadvantages. The criticism of tower blocks of flats is related to industrialized building, because the simple repetitiveness of identical floors stacked one above the other, and the high concentration of the building elements on site, lent themselves to an economic use of industrialized techniques.

Even here, it is necessary to qualify 'economic use'. In fact from a structural point of view, most industrialized systems are basically more expensive than traditional building. High-rise building in Britain qualified for additional subsidies because it was inherently more expensive than low-rise building. Working within the cost limits the result was that the general standards of finish tended to be reduced to balance the higher structural costs.

With the most common 'heavy' precast concrete unit systems there are further disadvantages, of a physical nature. The concrete in the units is so dense that unless fixings and fittings are cast into the units during manufacture the only way of providing fixings on site is by firing them in with an explosive tool. When it comes to hanging a picture in the living-room the problem is very real. And this highlights one of the long-term disadvantages: the lack of flexibility. The great advantage of the traditional brick-built house is that structurally, by its being made of small components, holes and openings can be formed fairly easily and cheaply and existing openings blocked up. Rearrangements can be made over the years. In this way many very old houses are adaptable to modernization. But what happens with a precast concrete block of flats in fifty years' time? You cannot remove complete panels without disturbing the basic structure; you cannot cut holes in the panels. In many cases even the replacement of services could pose a problem, and these tend to need replacement more than once during the lifetime of a building. There is a danger that these buildings will become the slums of the not too distant future, just as the late nineteenth-century tenements are at the moment. They may not be slums in the sense of overcrowded dwellings, but in terms of substandard housing, bearing in mind that acceptable or desired standards are rising rapidly, and will certainly be considerably higher well within the expected life of these buildings.

Of even greater concern than this is the whole question of the layout of housing schemes where industrialized systems have been used. While there are examples of well-planned layouts, the tendency is for tower blocks to be planned as independent units, with the intermediate spaces at ground level arrived at as a result of the application of daylighting standards, car-parking requirements, service access *and* the use of mechanical plant for construction. There is a strong tendency for tall blocks, even if not towers, to be built in distinct zones, and lower buildings, even where they are constructed in a similar manner, to be zoned separately rather than being closely linked together. The quality of the spaces, the social possibilities and needs of the community in the less tangible sense, go by default. This is really the basis of a concrete jungle.

I have mentioned that there are examples of well-planned layouts. In this country the Ministry of Housing and Local Government Research and Development Group has designed schemes using a particular industrialized system, and in fact helping to develop it, both in Oldham and in West Ham, in London. The Oldham scheme is of low-rise buildings laid out with great emphasis on the quality and usability of the open spaces as an essential part of the environment. Private architects working for the Greater London Council have designed a large scheme at Croydon using partly industrialized tall buildings, and partly two-storey houses built in a rationalized traditional way. Again, a high standard of layout has been achieved. It is nonetheless interesting to note that in all cases where this is so, the design has been firmly in the hands of independent professional consultants, and not in the hands of the building contractor.

The trouble has been that many local authorities, particularly the smaller ones which do not have their own well-qualified professional advisers, have accepted the package deal at the expense of the design. This was done with the blessing of the Government, which set up the National Building Agency to examine the various proprietary building systems and issue licences of approval to those which qualified. In the light of experience the policy of the NBA has changed over the years, but initially they were in the position of licensing complete systems, thereby encouraging building contractors to secure as much business as they could on a purely commercial basis in a market financed by the State, and whose requirements were often not of a commercial nature at all.

Despite all the criticism, there are so many advantages to industrialized building that we should consider its intrinsic possibilities very seriously. I discussed earlier the success of school building programmes derived from industrialized methods. The economic basis that I examined is quite relevant. What seems to be wrong with the approach so far are the assumptions that have been made as to the form that industrialization and industrialized building should take. There are three basic possibilities : (1) completely prefabricated building units, like the post-war prefabs; (2) complete building systems, like the schools or the systems used for housing; (3) coordinated modular components, which, like the bricks and timber of traditional building, can be assembled in a variety of ways. In a sense the tent is the earliest example of a prefabricated dwelling. In modern terms there have been numerous experiments in the form of the completely prefabricated dwelling, ranging from the caravan to Buckminster Fuller's Dymaxion house of the late 1920s, the post-war prefabs, units like Moshe Safdie's Habitat at the Montreal Expo 66, the ideas of the Archigram Group of 'plug-in cities' which themselves owe much to the concept of the space capsule.

The idea of the completely prefabricated unit is related to the potentials of an industry like the motor-car industry, which can mass-produce a complete working package, in its case a mobile unit incorporating many of the requirements of the living environment, though by no means all of them. The proponents of this approach suggest that housing should be treated in the same way as the motor-car, as a mechanized living environment which could be bought or rented as a complete package and 'plugged' in to a structural framework with all the main services. Unfortunately the concept tends to play down the basic inflexibility of such units by pointing to the degree of standardization of traditional housing forms, while at the same time ignoring the increasing tendency of motor manufacturers rigorously to reduce the number of their models in the interests of economy. However small the living unit might be, it is very much larger than the largest car, and much of it would be an enclosure for air. It is significant that the motor-car and the space capsule both reduce the volume enclosed to the absolute minimum; the larger package of the house would, I suspect, be disproportionately expensive however many new materials could be exploited. This would then raise the question of the economic life of the unit. The motor-car is designed for a limited lifespan, and measured in terms of space and equipment over this limited number of years, represents an extremely expensive cost, per cubic metre per annum, of useful life compared with even the most expensive house. As a result the 'package' house would have to have a much longer life than the car if it were to be economically feasible; yet the design and construction necessary to achieve this durability would simply add to the cost. Even allowing for the fact that the car is perhaps a more complex and sophisticated piece of machinery than the house (its engine, in fact, does not represent a particularly high percentage of its total cost), it does not seem that, even on technical grounds, such an approach is feasible within the foreseeable future, even if it were desirable on social and aesthetic grounds, which is highly questionable. That one can build complete units economically has been demonstrated by the post-war prefabs; but they were standardized to a degree which would not be generally acceptable, and were anyway single-storey structures, detached from each other. As a result there were few structural problems, few problems of fire separation from (i.e. protection between) adjoining dwellings, and the layout of the units was considered unimportant. To achieve the higher densities and cope with the technical problems, would make them very much more expensive, perhaps prohibitively so. Certainly the cost of units built in Montreal was far beyond what could be entertained for large-scale social housing programmes anywhere.

So far as the complete building systems are concerned, it is interesting that the schools systems have been successful whereas, in my opinion at least, the housing systems are unsuccessful. Several factors may account for this. The most important is undoubtedly the basis and method of design. The teams of designers who developed the schools systems were multi-discipline teams of specialists who examined the whole problem of basic school design as well as construction. They worked with manufacturers in the development of structures and components and followed a process of continuous reappraisal and development. In other words, the impetus and control came from designers, including architects, engineers, quantity surveyors and other specialists, and not from the building contractors. The final product was the result of careful planning and co-ordination between the designers and the manufacturers of the components and the structure. The building contractor's job was basically the preparation of the site and the co-ordination of the manufacturers who, to a large extent, installed their components themselves. Although these were complete building systems, which were not interchangeable with other systems, within themselves they were based upon a system of interchangeable components. To that extent they differed from the housing systems where the interchangeability of components even within the system was limited, since many of the components were actually part of the structure. The schools systems clearly separated the structure from the cladding and partitioning and thereby allowed a considerable measure of flexibility for future use, as well as for planning. The housing systems were designed mainly from a technical point of view, the criteria being found in the manufacturing process and site erection. In a sense, all that the builders were trying to do was to cut down the number of components involved regardless of function and other requirements. There was certainly not the study in depth which preceded and accompanied the development of the schools systems.

It may be argued that in some respects the schools systems were solving a simpler problem. Generally the buildings were not more than three storeys high, so that the structural system could be simpler than that used for housing, which could vary from two to twenty storeys. Yet by the same token one could claim that, despite

Georgian houses, Merrion
Square, Dublin.

Detail of the CLASP
school built as the
British pavilion at the
Milan Trienale, 1960.

Detail of the CLASP system used for York University (Robert Matthew, Johnson-Marshall & Partners, architects).

Essex University (Architects' Co-Partnership), 1966.

1950s housing: Roehampton, Surrey (GLC Architects' Department).

1950s housing: Park Hill, Sheffield (City Architects' Department).

variations in house types, there is a much greater consistency of structural span in housing than in schools, and inevitably less variety of general plan layout.

In fact, both the Ministry of Housing Research and Development Group and the National Building Agency, as well as other groups, have been studying in depth the problems of house building for some years, but only a limited amount had been done before the industrialized systems were introduced. Since then there has been a clear move in the direction of co-ordinated modular components as being the most fruitful approach to industrialized housing. The changeover to metric dimensions in the building industry is providing a timely and appropriate opportunity for developing the co-ordination of dimensions and standardization of components for housing, and a considerable amount of work is presently in progress on these lines.

The advantages of this approach are many. To begin with, the possibilities of interchangeability of components offer a freedom and flexibility of planning and design comparable to what can be achieved by traditional means. If one takes as an example eighteenth-century Georgian housing, some of the possibilities become clear. In general, Georgian houses were not designed individually, but built according to established proportions and dimensions, incorporating a considerable number of standard designs for windows, doors, fanlights, mouldings and ironwork which were taken from pattern books. It is by no means inconceivable that we could achieve a comparable standard of design and sophistication in modern terms by employing a similar approach. The charm and quality of Georgian houses lie largely in the good proportions, the rhythmic pattern of repeated units, the simplicity of materials, and a number of micro-variations in detail. Subject to the quality of design of a range of co-ordinated components, an equally high standard could be achieved today. The clear divorcing of structural components from external cladding and partitioning, as in the schools systems, would allow for a substantial degree of flexibility in the internal arrangement of spaces, and for long-term rearrangements. The same components could also be used regardless of the structure, height or size of the building. There would also be considerable scope for development, and future improvements in stan-

D

dards and service installations could be carried out without disturbing the basic structure of the building.

What is therefore required is a structural framework with main services, which can be geared to the general planning and social needs, with the rest of the fabric constructed of co-ordinated units and components. This suggests that in terms of planning and land allocation, certain spaces should be allocated to different types of housing, whether on the ground or in multi-storey structures, which could then be filled in with the various component parts, allowing a degree of flexibility within the allocated space. Serge Chermayeff and Christopher Alexander, in a book entitled *Community and Privacy,** have suggested something on these lines for single-storey housing, and a similar study has been carried out by the Thamesmead team of planners working at the GLC. In both cases it has been suggested that dwellings could expand and retract as a result of changing family circumstances within the allocated structural space. Theoretically this is possible, although the economic factors involved in additional or surplus components might preclude it. Equally, there are certain social assumptions inherent in that idea, concerning the mobility or otherwise of the family unit which may not accord with trends, present or future. Nevertheless, the possibilities are there, and demonstrate what could be achieved by such an approach.

The implications of developing the industrialization of building by co-ordinated modular components are wide. First, there is no reason for restricting the components to a particular type of building. There are enough elements common to all building types for the advantages to be utilized generally. Second, the role of the building contractor is likely to have to change and in turn the roles of the professional designers. The building contractor will need to become more and more a co-ordinator and assembler of components on site. He will have to develop greater skills in planning and programming, and will almost certainly begin to use the computer as a tool in the whole field of project management. The architect may well find himself having to choose between two important paths: (1) the overall planning of the building and the selection and incorporation of the components, and (2) the design of components,

* New York: Doubleday, 1963.

in which case he will move towards the role of the industrial designer. In both cases he will have to work in closer liaison with industry than he tends to do at present. There will also have to be many more development teams involved in the design of components, and it may be that these will evolve as independent design groups, acting partly as consultants to industry and partly as consultants to executive architects and planners.

There are probably other possibilities and computations, depending on the attitudes taken by government, the industry and the professions, and in a later chapter I will try to show how the professions may improve their service. There is no doubt that industrialization of building components and techniques will deeply affect their development. It has been argued correctly that the positive use of these developments could help to free the architect from many technical chores, and enable him to devote more time to his real *raison d'etre*, as a designer.

Chapter 6

Planning for an Urban Society

Our discussion of the mass building programmes and the problems of industrialized building, high-rise versus low-rise development, the commercial development of city centres and so on, brings us inevitably to the core of the present problems of planning. We have been guilty since 1945 of carrying out development on a piecemeal basis not so very far removed from that of the nineteenth century. We have set up systems of planning and control which are largely restrictive, and have only recently begun to appreciate the extent to which the national and international problems of economic, regional and physical planning, transport, housing, community development and so on are interdependent. We have, and are still committing blunders in building and development for which we may have to pay dearly in the not so distant future. We have reached a stage where problems of environmental pollution are becoming critical and the conservation of open space, countryside, wild-life not just desirable but essential for the future physical and mental health of society. So we must ask, what ideas and theories are under consideration for solving these problems? Can we afford the swings from one extreme to another, mentioned in connection with housing in the last chapter?

In his book *The World Cities*,[1] Peter Hall compares the seven great metropolitan areas of the world, summarizes some of the problems concerned with suburban spread and then makes the point that whatever the form of residential area that is planned, the ultimate factor which will make or break the city is the distribution of employment. As he says, it is this factor which determines the basic transport problems and the concentration at the centre of the

[1] London: Weidenfeld & Nicolson, World University Library, 1966.

city. It is this concentration which has been the origin of city growth from early times and which is still growing in most cities. The future urban problem is therefore whether decentralization of employment can or should be made to work, or whether the centralization should be continued and future planning geared to it.

There are technological possibilities that could make both alternatives feasible, to some extent at least. I stated in the first chapter that the history of the city is the history of communication in its widest sense. I also emphasized how the intense development of the city since the Industrial Revolution was dependent on communications, in particular physical communications. The present major problem of the city is also of physical communications. Yet the development of the technology of communications has enabled contact between people to be made without their physical, face-to-face presence. The introduction of postal services, the telegraph, telephone, radio and television have enabled more communication to to take place between people with less physical presence, and electronic means of communication are developing apace.

Yet far from easing the situation, the increased means of communication and increased complexity of the working life of an industrial society have meant that there is more information to be communicated and a greater demand for communication of ideas as society becomes more educated. The resultant growth of communications industries, advertising agencies, and the so-called media, together with the increasing demands of straightforward administrative communication in a consumer society, have intensified the centralization in the cities of these occupations, while the manufacturing industries have tended to decentralize. The extended governmental role in the social services, industry and general administration has added to this centralization. There are a number of planners who consider that the further development of communications media and sophisticated forms of transport may make possible and desirable complete decentralization of industry, distribution, administration and services, and that there could be, as a result, a much greater freedom in the choice of housing forms. They argue that hitherto we have always considered planning in terms of space and form, a physical structure within which the life and processes of industrial society are expected to fit. They suggest

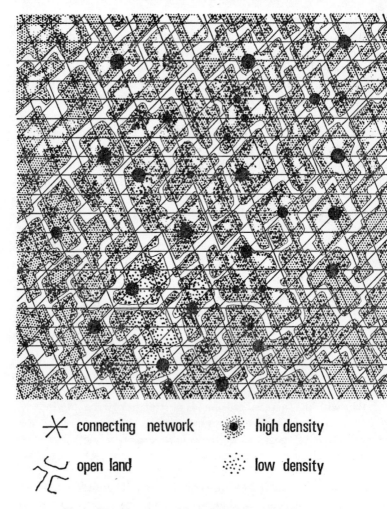

connecting network   high density

open land   low density

FIG. 11   Kevin Lynch's scheme for a dispersed metropolis

that we should adopt a new approach : analyse the processes of development themselves and then find appropriate forms to fit them. They then suggest how this can be done, usually setting out a structure, even though a tentative one.

In the United States both Kevin Lynch and Melvin Webber

have developed theories and suggestions along these lines. Kevin Lynch has developed a scheme for a dispersed metropolitan area based upon a triangular transport grid with high densities of development at the intersections and along the gridlines and low densities within the triangular spaces. The actual spacing of the gridlines would be closer towards the centre of the urban area, more open towards the periphery, and there would be belts of open land forming another type of grid, penetrating through the transport network (see Fig. 11). Within this network or grid the concentrations of development would form a sort of hierarchy of specialized urban functions. This would be achieved by the planners setting down the development grid for transport and communications, even applied to an existing rather than a virgin situation, and encouraging growth at the 'natural' development points, i.e. at the intersections. The existing functions of the central urban area would be encouraged to disperse into specialized areas at these points, so that the different functions would be spread over the whole urban area. Formal land zoning and density control would be utilized as little as possible, and more to control the form of development than the actual uses of land. In other words, the 'natural' and economic forces would be allowed to determine the detailed pattern of development within a flexible framework laid down by the planners. Webber does not go so far as Lynch in laying down a planning grid. He is concerned that we should determine the correct social organization for the urban area and then let the spatial organization follow in a logical way, accepting that the patterns of land use and density will become as complex as the patterns of society.

These theories embody a conscious reaction against the traditional European approach to the problem and to the idea of the city, and are a natural product of the American environment and culture. They represent a sort of nineteenth-century *laissez-faire* approach controlled by the techniques of social study and analysis which were not available to the Victorians. They are closely related to the economic structure of American society and must be considered in this light. They are also related to the fact that population density in the United States is generally much lower than in the urban countries of Western Europe and that there is already a predominance of dispersed urban development and widespread private transport. It may well be that, given the space, the 'natural' tendency of the British would be for a similar dispersal, since in Britain there seems to be an inherent preference for suburban living, although one must question the historical reasons for this and whether increased living standards and greater national security may produce a tendency towards a similar desire in Europe generally. However, the problems of European cities are to some extent different, so that it seems doubtful whether the American approach would be feasible on this side of the Atlantic.

The biggest question posed by this approach lies in the economic assumptions. In the long run it would mean that those members of society, whether individually or corporately, who succeeded in economic terms, would have the first choice of places to live and work, and those who did not succeed economically would have to make do with the leftovers. It would confirm that economic factors were the decisive ones in a social structure, and indeed in the whole culture of society. If, following Webber's arguments, it is agreed that this is not the ideal, and that the distribution of land, for that is what is at stake, should follow a more egalitarian social pattern, then one inevitably returns to a pattern of land use and control which must cut across the so-called natural patterns that would result from purely economic considerations. It is conceivable that economic models could be constructed which allowed not only for a straightforward capital cost against return process, but for hidden costs and returns which would arise from a particular development. But this kind of attempt to quantify social costs and assets would be highly questionable. However, assuming that it were possible and reasonable, then the pattern which would emerge would be one of land-value control, and its effect might not be very different from the type of land-use control that exists at present. At present the value of land is determined largely by the use and density for which it is zoned; the alternative would ultimately determine its use by its value. Perhaps what we should be looking for is a combination of the two, whereby a possible or apparently desirable land use could be checked against the capital and social costs of its development. To some extent this exercise is being undertaken in the much criticized 'motorway box' planning by the GLC.

It is still difficult to predict in economic terms what would be the advantages or disadvantages to society, since these can only be measured in terms of a projection of existing situations and cannot take into account future technical and social changes. Perhaps in the age of the computer such techniques will reach a stage of sophistication where all is predictable. Certainly we have not yet reached that stage and meanwhile we have to produce solutions to urgent problems. We must conclude, therefore, that the ideas of Lynch and Webber may be applicable to the capitalist society that exists at present in the United States, assuming that American society continues along its present path of development. I am doubtful of their effectiveness even in that highly volatile society. In my view, if we accepted their approach we would be trying in effect to escape from certain basic decisions and value judgments about society and to substitute a questionable materialistic objectivity.

Constantine Doxiadis has developed a planning grid which has a certain similarity to Kevin Lynch's, except that his is rectangular rather than triangular. He has developed ideas of planning into a total concept which he has called 'Ekistics' and which is intended to embrace all the considerations affecting physical and social planning. His approach involves a large team of specialists in various fields, and his work has been undertaken largely in the developing countries of Africa and in Pakistan. His planning grid is a transport grid, the closest spacing of which is on 1-kilometre squares in urban areas with motorway routes at multi-kilometre intervals, some of which then extend into rural areas, so creating a network on a national scale. In the urban area each enclosed kilometre square contains a specific urban function; in the case of residential areas it would be a neighbourhood unit.

In physical terms Doxiadis' approach bears a close resemblance to Corbusier's ideas, and particularly to Corbusier's plan for Chandigarh in India. While it has a formal similarity to Lynch's plan, it is not conceived from the same point of view. It is a much more controlled situation in which a series of social assumptions are made from the outset and in which the idea of land-use control and zoning is used to select the best areas for particular functions in relation to (a) topography, climate and orientation, (b) inter-urban transport, and (c) the overall form of the urban area, i.e. the relation of its parts

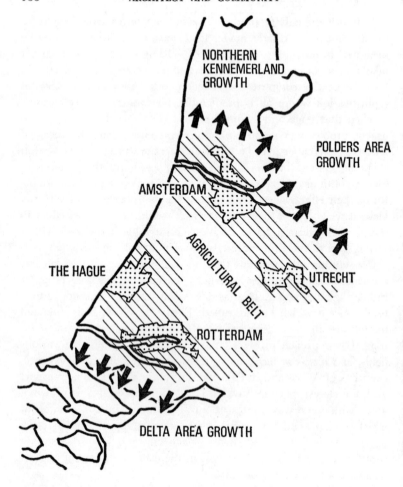

FIG. 12 Randstad conurbations, Holland

to a central core. Its inflexibility is apparent in relation to existing urban areas which are not planned on a regular rectangular grid, but it is to some extent adaptable. In the countries where most of his work is being done Doxiadis' planning may be more effective, since he is starting from less developed areas.

The other aspect of the Lynch/Webber ideas, the decentralization of the metropolitan area into a *polycentric* rather than a concentric area, can be seen developing in at least two European countries, without the *laissez-faire* attitudes that accompany the American approach. In Holland, the most densely populated country in Europe, the urban areas around the cities of Rotterdam, The Hague, Amsterdam and Utrecht are being developed by the planners as a polycentric metropolitan area called Randstad (Ring City) in the form of a horseshoe around an agricultural area. In effect the planners are taking hold of a situation that was developing and guiding it along clearer lines. The western part of Holland was developing as the most important industrial area, while at the same time being an important agricultural area. The development of industry and the movement of population from the land into the urban areas were creating pressures on land, particularly for housing in an area where the population density was anyway over 2,000 per square mile (compared with an average of 772 in England and Wales), in 1960. Dutch planning policy for this area is to develop towns outside the ring in such a way as to relieve the population growth of the Randstad itself; to preserve the individual identity of the historical cities themselves; to allow for future expansion along transport lines radiating from Randstad and in particular in re-claimed areas to the north-east and south-west; to preserve the agricultural 'heartland' at all costs. There are also plans in Germany for a large polycentric urban area embracing the cities of the Ruhr.

The important thing about the polycentric concept is that it enables employment to be decentralized while at the same time preserving and even accentuating the identity of existing cities. It is in fact an example of part of the Lynch/Webber thesis applied to an existing situation, and it may be one of the most fruitful possibilities for the major urban areas of Western Europe and the United States. It could be applied, for example, to the urban areas of the Midlands, South Lancashire, Yorkshire, the Tees and Glasgow/Edinburgh, since the situation is similar to those in Holland and Germany. London presents a more difficult problem, since it is such a vast single centre. The attempted decentralization of the New Town programme had a similar aim to the Dutch plan, except that the secondary centres were disproportionately

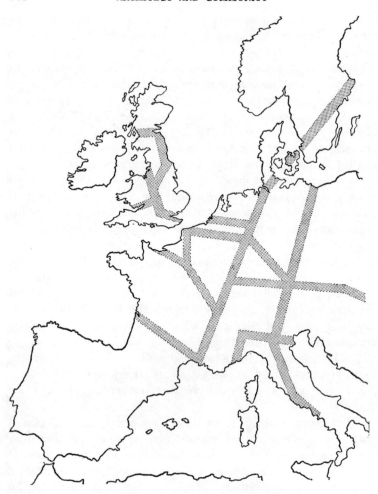

FIG. 13   Possible future European conurbation links

smaller than the main one. Inevitably, building a ring of satellite towns will tend to accentuate the concentric nature of London as the central magnet of the South East, unless those satellites begin to approach the size and magnetizing potential of London itself.

Approaches have been suggested on a much grander scale and

with longer term projections which might, it is claimed, offer solutions in the polycentric pattern. One of these examines the problem on an international, or continental scale. Taking the major transport routes of Western Europe which link the major urban areas, it envisages a linear development of urban areas, somewhat on the Randstad pattern, along these routes. In these terms there would be a major urban area, including London, stretching from the Midlands to the Kent coast and on the other side of the Channel onwards to Paris. There is much to be said for this approach, particularly at a time when the extension of the European Economic Community to include Britain, and part at least of Scandinavia, is likely to take place. This fact alone would make it desirable to begin to examine urban development in Europe on an international basis. Movements in this direction are already taking place, namely in the plans for Paris and its expansion westwards towards Le Havre, taking into its planned polycentric urban area the important town of Rouen.

If the enlarged European Economic Community is economically successful the expansion of industry and the natural increase in population will demand considerable extension in urban development. It may well be that the scale of expansion will only be controllable in a pattern of linear urban areas forming a network over the whole area. The alternative would be that vast areas would be developed as a suburban sprawl, with complex and difficult transport routes and a loss, almost total in many areas, of open countryside. Quite possibly these proposals, huge in scale as they appear, will provide the only way of conserving the elements of the environment which are most vulnerable to urban development.

The opposing concepts of the concentric and polycentric approach to planning have become apparent over recent years in the more detailed consideration of town planning. The concentric concept was the basis of Ebenezer Howard's ideas, which in turn stemmed from the traditional concept of the town. The pre-industrial city was a relatively simple centre for a region, basically agricultural, and provided marketing and administrative services. The city of the industrial era has become a much more complex organism both within itself and in relation to its surrounding region. In fact the surrounding region may well be the whole country in so far as the products of the industrial city, its administrative and communication needs, are no longer restricted to a relatively small surrounding region. It is the combination of many such cities that creates a complex, interlinked and interdependent communication network over the whole country, and now increasingly on a continental scale.

The further complication brought about by motor transport is that it provides a flexible, door-to-door means of communication, so that the complex national network is repeated on a smaller and smaller scale until it affects every part of the urban environment. The congestion occurs where this flexible system, which theoretically allows everyone to travel door to door by the shortest route, is channelled into a road network based on pre-industrial means of transport.

In 1963 a report on the long-term encroachment of motor traffic in urban areas in Britain was published. The study leading to the report was commissioned in 1960 by the then Minister of Transport and the latter has become known as the Buchanan Report, after Colin Buchanan, a traffic engineer and town planner who was appointed to lead the Working Group in the Ministry which prepared the report, known officially as *Traffic in Towns*. The report studied the problems inherent in a society in which the majority of families would own at least one car, the effect of this scale of ownership on the growth of towns, the implications in terms of road building, the possible need for restriction of cars in towns and the effects on and development of public transport.

Britain is an excellent example of a country whose roads are based on pre-industrial patterns, whose towns and cities are concentric in form, where there are conurbations of industrial cities forming large sprawling urban areas, and where there is a fairly dense network of transport routes over the whole area. As yet, it is about a generation behind the United States in the level of car ownership, so that some of the effects of the higher levels of ownership can be studied and the British situation projected at least a few years ahead. *Traffic in Towns* suggested three short-term measures and one long-term measure. The short-term ones were: the building of urban motorways (as distinct from inter-urban motorways); the restriction of the number of cars in city centres

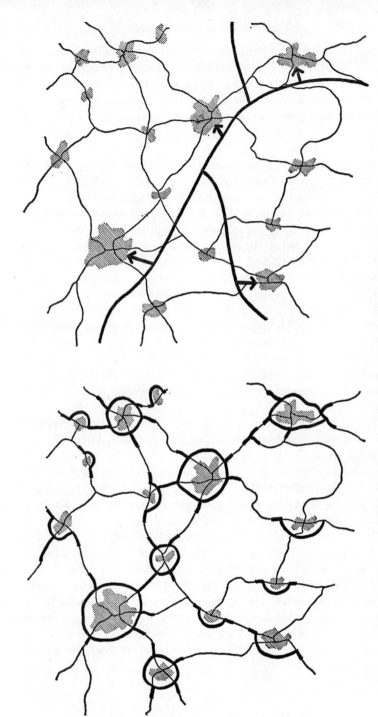

FIG. 14 Colin Buchanan's skeletal road system (right) beside an existing bypass system

either by taxation or licensing; the development and expansion of public transport. The long-term measure was replanning our towns by means of regional agencies, with powers to co-ordinate the plans of all the local authorities in the region, and ensure that the towns and cities were preserved as good places to live in while at the same time allowing the greatest freedom and ease of movement for traffic.

Buchanan went further than this and considered in detail the problems and possibilities of replanning by studies of a small provincial town, part of an industrial conurbation, and a section of central London. In his studies certain conclusions were reached. First, in looking at the problem of inter-urban transport and how to stop it from destroying the smaller towns and villages, he came out against the traditional policy of 'bypassing', since the encircling bypass ring would tend to restrict growth, in time become overloaded and would anyway take through traffic closer than necessary and involve it in local traffic routes. He proposed instead that motorways or major roads should have spur access to towns and villages but should otherwise steer clear of them (see Fig. 14). This can be interpreted as a clear step towards the polycentric concept of planning, since it would enable the development and growth of centres along a main transport route without blocking that route.

In later studies of development plans Buchanan has developed this idea into what have been called 'linear' towns. Essentially this is the polycentric theory in practice. In developing the replanning ideas for existing urban areas Buchanan, like other planners, has adopted a transport grid as the ideal, his grid being hexagonal, which form, he claims, gives a good distribution with comparatively simple intersections. He also establishes a hierarchy, of what he calls 'distributor' roads. These are distinct from inter-urban roads on the one hand, and local access roads on the other. The hierarchy is on the basis of a town or primary network broken down into district and local distributors. Together with these he establishes the concept of the environmental area as the 'rooms' of the town, where traffic may be considerable but only concerned with that area. This is distinct from the concept of the traffic-free precinct. The grid as a regular geometrical pattern would be used in the case of an

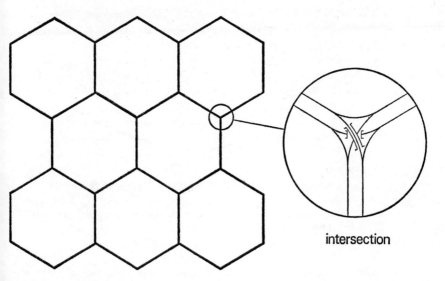

intersection

FIG. 15 A hexagonal transport grid for urban areas proposed by Colin Buchanan.

extensive area with a uniform spread of development. He demonstrates his ideas in relation to specific areas, and also in relation to time scales. In other words he shows how improvements can be made without total redevelopment, but how these improvements relate in turn to future possibilities of further development. He advocates multi-level planning in city centres in order to permit freedom of movement for both pedestrian and vehicle without destroying the quality of the environmental area.

The polycentric idea has been stretched to one extreme in the form of what has been called the linear city, which has virtually no centres at all, and is a continuous development along a major transport route. Such an idea was suggested as long ago as 1882 by Arturo Soria y Mata, who wrote that the ideal city would be 'a single street unit 500 metres broad, extending if necessary from Cadiz to St Petersburg, from Peking to Brussels'. In 1910, Edgar Chambless designed a continuous concrete house of indefinite length with trains in the basement and a pedestrian way on the

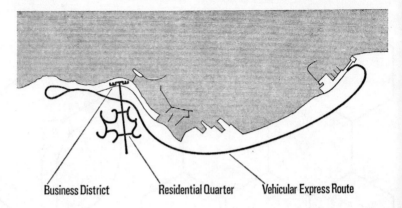

Business District   Residential Quarter   Vehicular Express Route

FIG. 16   An early study for a linear town: Le Corbusier's and P. Jeanneret's 'Shrapnel' project—Algiers, 1930

roof.[2] Corbusier made a project for 'road building' in Rio de Janeiro in 1929 and in Algiers in 1930-4. The recent Archigram 'plug-in city' is in the same tradition.

It would seem to me that these ideas are naïve in so far as they overemphasize an already powerful element and make of it the paramount criterion of the urban environment. However important transport and communications have been and still are, they are but one element, or one tool, for establishing the relationships between people that make up a society. American experience bears out this point and the views of American planners are interesting in comparison with their European counterparts. Elizabeth Kassler, commenting upon the recent interest in the linear town, free movement and non-finite urbanization in Europe, in an introduction to an exhibition, 'The New City: Architecture and Urban Renewal' held at the Museum of Modern Art in 1967, wrote: 'So Europe arrives at a place we know well: the no-place of mobility and noncentricity, the no-place like home. The full circle is accomplished. . . .'

The proponents of the linear concept are in fact reacting against

[2] Edgar Chambless, 'Project for Roadtown' (1910), from *Sunset, the Pacific Monthly* (January 1914), shown at the exhibition, 'The New City: Architecture and Urban Renewal', Museum of Modern Art, New York (January-March 1967).

planning and towards the *laissez-faire* attitudes we have already found in certain American planners. It is also interesting that these ideas are the product, in Europe at least, of a purely architectural and technological outlook. Social and political considerations are conspicuously left out, and one cannot help wondering how far this represents the architect fighting to impose his ideas on a society which already realizes that this is not his exclusive province any more.

Examples of the more limited view of the linear town, which would fit in ultimately more closely with the concept of the poly-centric urban area, can be found in Cumbernauld New Town and Livingston New Town in Scotland, and in the project planned, but unfortunately not executed, for a new town at Hook in Hampshire, by the Greater London Council. Buchanan's plan for the Portsmouth-Southampton urban area is a clear example of his ideas on these lines.

All these examples are based upon a reassessment of the problems as a result of the lessons of the earlier new towns, which were concentric in form, and as a result were found to be difficult to expand to the extent that clearly became necessary in the late 'fifties and 'sixties. The *South East Study*, published by the Ministry of Housing and Local Government in 1964, which examined 'the problems that may be expected to arise in South-East England over the next twenty years, as a result of the big growth and movements of population that are likely to take place', highlighted the particular growth problems of the new towns. The conclusions of this report are interesting and worth quoting :

So far as the basic problem is concerned, there is little choice; large population increases in the South East are inevitable. Twenty-year forecasts can go badly wrong; but present evidence suggests that if the estimates in this Study prove to be inaccurate, they will be shown to be under-estimates.

Where the choice does lie is in the type of plan to deal with the population increase. The Study, while recognizing the strength of the economic forces which are leading to more and more growth in the London area, takes as its main principle the decentralization of population and employment. The aim is to break the vicious circle of growth generating more growth in the most crowded and congested part of the South East—not only the London conurbation itself, but the ring around it, which has been experiencing the fastest population growth of any part of the country. . . . This would make a start on the road towards a more even distribution of population growth in the South East; and, as the new big cities built up, the change in the pattern of population growth would be reinforced by a gradual shift in the economic balance within the South East.

These conclusions demonstrate a clear acceptance of the poly-centric concept as the only feasible answer to the problems of the South East. The main problem in this policy will be the enormous imbalance between London and any other even fully developed city in the region. To this extent the problem is more difficult than that in Holland and it remains to be seen how successful the policy will prove. Buchanan's plan for Portsmouth-Southampton and a number of other plans for expanded towns were a direct result of the *South East Study,* so the general direction, in physical terms, is being spelled out quite clearly.

The interesting thing is that when one gets to the problem of the city centre, there seems to be little basic disagreement among planners as to how the solutions shall be effected. Buchanan's ideas in detail do not differ very much from those of Victor Gruen in the United States, although their ideas on town planning generally seem to be at opposite ends of the pole, Gruen being a staunch advocate of the concentric pattern firmly rooted in the tradition of Ebenezer Howard. Both accept the need for mixed development, much advocated by Jane Jacobs in *The Death and Life of Great American Cities.* It is also generally accepted that the unrestricted use of private cars in city centres cannot be tolerated much longer anywhere, and that the best method of restriction is to provide a cheap, comfortable and effective public transport system which will be preferred to the motor-car.

However, although there may be general agreement among the planners on these points, even if there are deep disagreements else-where, there does not yet seem to be the political awareness neces-sary to put into effect powers enabling the planners to carry out

their schemes. And by political awareness I mean essentially awareness on the part of the public as a whole, to the extent of forcing
the politicians to take effective action. The pressure on politicians
comes at present from sources which tend to ignore the dangers
facing the quality of the urban environment in favour of commercial
expediency. In a country where the motor industry plays a dominant role in exports, an industry which insists that the home market
must be expanded if exports are to continue, and where the national
economic situation demands increased exports, then the politicians
in power will tend to follow the dictates of that industry. The result
will be what is presently happening in this country : the construction
of an increasing number of inter-urban motorways; the construction
and planning of a number of urban motorways and ring roads
without relation to the general planning needs of the particular city;
reliance on an increasingly ineffective method of reducing the
number of cars in central city districts by means of parking restrictions; and pressure to make public transport 'pay its way' in
commercial terms while leaving it to operate in conditions where
this is virtually impossible. At least until recently there was a strong
government programme of economic help to relatively under-
developed areas in order to encourage the decentralization of industry and commerce. Under the present Tory Government it is by
no means certain that this programme will be maintained; and if
it is dropped, there will be a tendency for ever-increasing centralization of jobs in the big cities which will further aggravate the transport situation.

There is no simple remedy. It is not just a question of the
planners being right, nor even of local government requirements.
It depends on the basic direction taken by certain industries which
are key industries in terms of the economy and the environment.
Indeed, it will probably mean a reconsideration of many economic
assumptions governing the investment in redevelopment generally
and which in turn will involve the whole question of the direction
of capitalist society.

It may be suggested that the motor industry diversifies so as not
to be so dependent on the sale of private cars; but in what direction?
It will probably have to look for new products or to industrializing
hitherto un-industrialized processes, like the building industry.

Equally it would help if people generally regarded their cars as items of capital investment, rather than as status symbols or toys.

I have already suggested that the cost of buying and running the average family car approaches that of buying and running a house. Yet on average the car is driven probably for less than 10 per cent of the time during which it could be used (on the basis of a sixteen-hour period per day). In commercial terms the use of a capital item of equipment for so limited a time would be unthinkable. It could justifiably be argued that this is a waste we cannot afford in a period when we do not have enough money for many essentials. The introduction of extremely cheap, if not free, public transport paid for out of taxation, plus a system of cheap private hire, self-drive cars and taxis established as a part of a national transport policy, might lead to a more sensible use of resources and achieve better results. The private car is invaluable for what may be called random journeys, in terms of a road network; because of the regular intense flows it causes, it is not satisfactory for commuting purposes. Some form of individual unit of transport, which could be controlled to link up with others into a particular regulated flow, is a possible alternative. An electronically controlled car could work in this fashion and serve both functions—for business and pleasure. Experiments on this and other more communal forms of public transport are being carried out with mounting pressure in many parts of the world as the situation becomes more serious.

There will undoubtedly be new forms of transport in the near future which may help to make the problem of planning our cities easier, but it must be stressed that whatever the form of vehicle or system the basic problems remain the same, and they will not be solved by a new feat of technological development.

This brings us to the core of the whole problem of the quality of the environment. However important transport and communications may have been historically, however vital the solution of the problems they pose today, and however important the decentralization of work-places and the need for integrating the various functions of the city rather than zoning them, the quality of the city will ultimately depend on the quality of the buildings we design, the spaces between those buildings and the way the buildings and spaces relate to each other and to the functions they must perform.

So far in this chapter we have looked at the basic functional requirements on the broadest level. The possibilities of meeting these are good on the professional level, poor on the political level, but how satisfying will they be if they are exploited without the visual awareness and sensitivity that are increasingly necessary as in turn the solutions to the problems become still more powerful elements in the environment?

One of the indirect products of the Buchanan Report in London is the Covent Garden Redevelopment Area. This area, bounded on the east by Kingsway, on the west by Charing Cross Road, on the south by the Strand and on the north by High Holborn, contains a wide variety of activities: the fruit and vegetable market, and its associated enterprises, the Royal Opera House and other theatres, general commercial concerns ranging from small shops to large office blocks, late nineteenth-century housing in the form of tenement blocks, hospital buildings, a swimming-pool, restaurants and so on. The redevelopment plan, starting from the decision to remove the fruit and vegetable markets from central London, offered a unique possibility for the imaginative redevelopment of an historic area full of life and character. Early on, there seemed a real chance of an exciting plan emerging, but political disagreements between the local government authorities involved, arising out of a lack of a clear overall policy for central London and of awareness of the needs of the existing community, have led to a half-hearted plan owing much to Buchanan's ideas but overemphasizing the role of private transport and commercial development to an extent where there is a very real danger of producing yet another sterile commercial development on a vast scale. The full possibilities of a careful balance between renovation of existing buildings and new development, phased in line with predictable social and functional changes in the area, seem to have been ignored in favour of a more conventional and rigidly phased physical redevelopment plan.

Is it possible to sum up the present situation in planning? The situation is fluid and many of the ideas frankly experimental, but certain lines are fairly clear.

(1) The post-1945 period has seen three basic approaches to the planning of urban areas for expansion :-

    (i) the relatively uncontrolled sprawl related to private car mobility as in Los Angeles;
    (ii) the concentric pattern of development as a result of the Ebenezer Howard tradition in the British New Towns, and in other parts of the world;
    (iii) the polycentric approach of the Dutch and German planners in Randstad and the Ruhr towns.

(2) A general acknowledgment by planners that the future quality of the city centre depends amongst other things upon :-

    (i) the restriction of the use of the private car;
    (ii) the development of improved public transport;
    (iii) the segregation of pedestrians from vehicles.

(3) A general acceptance that the concentration of employment in relatively few large cities, in a society where population is expanding, creates a vicious circle of growth promoting growth with the by-product of increasing congestion in movement; hence the need for decentralization of employment.

(4) A general acceptance that the rigidity of planning legislation in zoning for different activities is not planning, but tends to destroy the life of the city.

Beyond this one can say that of the three basic approaches to planning, concentric planning in the Howard tradition seems to be on the wane, since it does not appear to offer the solutions appropriate to the problems. Whether there is a positive approach to planning depends on political and economic factors, but it is likely that we shall see more and more strongly the development of the poly-centric urban area as the only viable and acceptable alternative to a general suburban sprawl on the one hand, or cities becoming ever more densely built and congested so that they virtually burn themselves up, on the other. The totally linear city will probably remain in the realm of fantasy, but the continentally orientated polycentric urban area may well become a reality.

Chapter 7

There's No Place Like Home

The truism 'there's no place like home' has real meaning for most people. For some of those involved in current building programmes, however, it seems to have no place in their working philosophy.

Under the pressures of an acute housing shortage, out-of-date schools and insufficient hospitals and universities we are rushing to provide more buildings as quickly as available resources permit. We are also concerned with improving the standards of the buildings we are planning, and with the problems of town planning, the integration of traffic within our towns in a rational way, in fact with many of the problems connected with the increasing inadequacy of our urban environment. We study the symptoms of social inadequacy and we talk at great length about social problems, and the need for better *homes*, but we have not yet learnt to consider, let alone apply, one simple principle. That principle can be expressed in the definition of 'home'. When most of us speak of 'home' we do not refer simply to a specific house, but to a locality, to the other houses and people around us, very often of the place where we grew up. The principle we have to accept, therefore, is that the place we call home is a combination of physical and social environment, the interplay of which may create either a stimulating, satisfying background for people or a dull and frustrating one. It is the quality of the physical aspects of 'place' and the opportunities for social life and activity offered which will largely determine how good a home we provide.

It follows that the physical and social aspects of the community must be considered simultaneously when any development is envisaged. It also follows that *all* the physical aspects and *all* the social aspects must be integrated if we are to plan a satisfactory home or neighbourhood for a community and its various activities.

Unfortunately, today all the social building programmes are administered, financed and planned by separate and specialist agencies. Any real chance of integrated planning based on a concept of a community as a home for a group of people and their activities is virtually impossible. The agency with the biggest voice will win the inevitable competition which arises, and if no one wins, this usually means that each one keeps carefully to its own confines and avoids treading on another's toes.

The fragmentation of society's needs for buildings into isolated and specialized groups which are dealt with piecemeal and in isolation from each other is wrong. A cultured and civilized society can only exist where all of men's activities have a real significance and free interplay; where a man's working hours are not merely used to earn his daily bread but are a worth-while part of his life in their own right. I believe that a man's life should not be treated as a series of stages—childhood, adolescence, young manhood, middle age, old age—that are isolated from each other, but as a steady transition and growth amongst other men. I am therefore opposed to any system which segregates ages, activities and groups, as much as I am opposed to a system of racial or religious segregation. I also oppose the way we plan our environment to further such segregation.

Historically speaking, the system of zoning the various functions of an area of human habitation into separate localities is relatively new. In the past, villages, towns and cities have all had in common the provision of facilities for the full range of human activity in a relatively concentrated area. The old cities which we think of as providing a stimulating and lively environment, such as Paris, Amsterdam or Venice, share this attribute with the traditional English village or market-town. The breakdown of the environment comes when one activity so predominates that it either forces the others out or makes them impossible. In a sense we can say that the activity of moving about in motor-cars is already destroying Paris and Amsterdam as it has destroyed many an English village. Venice, by virtue of its physical make-up, has avoided this fate, but is in danger of dying as a fully integrated city since it cannot cater satisfactorily for modern commercial and industrial activities.

Under the present system not only are factories and work-places, housing, commercial functions, markets, cultural, administrative and educational functions each allocated their own separate zones, but the buildings within each zone are treated as the exclusive domain of one, and only one, function, and often of one section of the community. Children are rigorously segregated for most of their active hours during at least ten years of their lives. The adult working population is segregated from all others for at least forty hours a week. Readers of books and drinkers of coffee never normally mix in the same building. Drinkers of alcohol are almost completely segregated from everyone else. Yet surely engagement in one activity does not of itself demand segregation from all others.

As Jane Jacobs has pointed out in her book *The Death and Life of Great American Cities* the vitality of the city street is largely a product of continuous and varying activities taking place in close proximity at all hours. Work-places, shops, restaurants, pubs, offices and housing are mixed up in such a way that there is always life and social activity. One has but to look at the City of London at the week-end or a suburban street in the evening to appreciate how dead an area of human habitation can be.

Of course, nobody wants to live all the time in an atmosphere of continuous bustle and hurly-burly. Quiet and privacy are essential requirements for satisfactory living conditions. It is both necessary and possible to provide for both. But this does not necessarily mean that housing areas should be planned exclusively for housing and separated by a twenty-minute walk from shops, pubs, restaurants, cinemas and libraries on the one hand, and an even longer walk to the factory work-place on the other, as in many of our new towns. It *does* mean, among other things, segregating motor-vehicles in a rational way, which those same new towns have largely failed to do.

Today there is no reason for a rigid segregation of work-places into industrial or business and commercial zones. In fact, in terms of transport alone, there is every reason for dezoning in order to avoid the great commuter problem. But apart from this, factories are not the 'dark satanic mills' they used to be, and generally they could well form part of a more varied community. Nothing can be more dreary than the industrial estate so beloved of our planners.

Except perhaps for heavy industries and chemical plants the bulk of modern industrial installations can be orderly, well designed and quiet. Once the segregation of motor-vehicles is accepted, servicing and transport present no problems. There is therefore no reason why factories should not be integrated into areas of housing together with schools and other community buildings. In the proposals for a new town at Hook, made by the Architects' Department of the LCC in 1961, a step was taken in this direction. Housing areas were to form fingers leading to a central spine of community buildings. Industry was to be located at the extremities of the fingers rather than being grouped in one industrial area. Regrettably, Hook remains a plan on paper and will not be built. Nevertheless, its influence as an idea is noticeable in recent planning schemes, so there is some hope that we may yet take a step in the right direction.

Similarly, there is no reason for the rigorous segregation of business and commercial buildings. Many of the most successful large buildings in the centres of the world's cities contain a mixture of shops, restaurants, offices and flats. The Rockefeller Center in New York is one such example from the 1930s. And latterly in the centre of Cumbernauld New Town, as in several recent proposals for town centre redevelopments, steps in the right direction have been taken. Even so conservative a body as the Corporation of the City of London has appreciated the deadening effect of a city's having one predominant function. The Barbican scheme is a comprehensive development which aims to incorporate housing, concert-hall, theatre and art gallery into an otherwise almost exclusively business area. But it is not enough to apply this principle only to the centres of our towns and cities. If it is valid there, it is also valid throughout the areas we build for the community.

It is not only necessary to question the conventional zoning of functions, which is a form of segregation of activities, but also the splitting up of groups within the community. The separation of old people's dwellings in areas apart from other housing is no longer held as a viable precept. But we still accept as natural and necessary that children should be segregated for considerable periods in schools. This practice tends inevitably to isolate the school from the community and helps to provoke the anti-school reaction of many a teenager. So much of our education is tied up with literacy that a good library should be considered as one of the most important facilities for a school. Yet comparatively few school libraries are sufficiently well stocked, while many public libraries are more than adequate for general requirements and relatively little used during the day. It should be possible to combine school and public library, allowing adults and pupils to mingle at any hour of the day or evening. This would help to break down some of the present barriers in an economical way.

In New Haven, Connecticut, a community school run on these lines is included in every urban renewal area. The Conte School, Wooster Square, for example, remains open after teaching hours for public recreation and social activities. Here the public library and club-rooms are arranged on either side of an open courtyard. The swimming-pool and gymnasium are available for public use and even the courtyard is fully utilized with chess-tables and a bowling-alley.

In Britain, as far back as the 1930s, we had an example of a multi-functional building in the Peckham Pioneer Health Centre. This provided facilities for medical and social research, a community health centre (in the days before the National Health Service) and a community social centre for local families. The centre was run and financed by the families and was freely open to members all day and all evening. Its canteen was run on self-service lines, not as a commercial expedient but following the principle that people should do things for themselves and not rely on being served by others. Doctors have already put forward the idea of the 'day hospital', which would be used by people who are able to move around and look after themselves generally but require regular medical attention, in place of the present in-patients system. The linking of such hospital facilities with a Peckham-type centre might help to ease or eliminate the fears most people have about going to a hospital. The modern hospital has become a vast centre for disease which is difficult to fit satisfactorily into the community either psychologically or physically.

These are but isolated examples of the way in which buildings, that we normally think of as housing one activity, could be used for a range of activities and thus help to bring different groups of people together. There are many similar possibilities. We must learn to think of buildings not as separate, specialist entities but as focal points, meeting-places for everyone in the community. We must then consider how to link housing and commercial functions to these focal points in such a way that together they form one entity. Venice is in effect one great building; so are hundreds of old villages throughout the world. This quality seems to be deeply satisfying to most people, who regard it nostalgically while resigning themselves to its impossibility in our modern world. But it is not impossible. Rather it is essential that we re-create this quality if we regard it as valuable.

One of the essential elements of this whole concept is that every part of the environment we build is to be lived in, in some way or other. We cannot afford to relegate any part as a dead area. We tend today to think of living areas as being restricted to the house or flat. We even describe the main room as the 'living-room'. Outside, the 'living-spaces' we create are severely compartmentalized. We may have a garden, even called an outdoor living-space, connected to the house. Otherwise we have streets, solely for circulation, play-spaces and open recreation areas generally classified as 'public open spaces', but which in fact are often public dead spaces. We seem to forget that we are alive all the time and that we can live as actively and consciously outdoors as indoors. As it is, the facilities and amenities provided and the way the spaces are planned tend to make many of our everyday outdoor activities dull if not positively unpleasant. The British bemoan or speak constantly about their variable and inclement weather. Yet, as in the old days of draughty houses and dusty coal-fires, we behave like masochists and seem unable to protect ourselves from rain or cold except for an occasional ineffective bus-shelter and a multitude of eye-damaging umbrellas. But means of providing sheltered walkways, covered shopping precincts, sheltered spaces for sitting, talking, having a drink out of doors, could be found easily and economically.

Once we have accepted the need for segregating motor-vehicles from pedestrians and that it is not essential to be able to *drive* right up to one's front door, it is feasible to think of pedestrian ways being *covered* right up to the front door. These covered ways could open out to provide play areas, sheltered sitting areas and even small market areas, housing the local shops as kiosks rather than as more elaborate buildings. Street furniture could be 'built-in' and the clutter of the modern street avoided. The covered ways could link up with bus-stops and garages so that one could always walk in shelter to one's house. One could also 'pop out' to the corner shop for a packet of cigarettes when it was raining without having to dress up to face the weather. Suggestions have been made that develop this idea to the extent of totally enclosing a city within a transparent umbrella and producing a controlled climate in the enclosure. It would then be unnecessary ever to face the variations of a natural climate. Buckminster Fuller, an American engineer and designer, has invented a structure by which such a city enclosure would be feasible, and the idea has been presented and discussed amongst certain architects and planners in all seriousness. It is against such simplistic solutions, with all their nightmarish science-fiction qualities, that we must guard ourselves, just as we must resist the unco-ordinated planning of the present.

My idea of covered ways is much more in the form of the Rows of Chester, or the arcaded streets of Bologna where one can walk and shop under cover without being totally isolated from the outdoor weather. But try walking from your house in Harlow New Town across the windswept wastes to the shopping centre and even around the shopping centre itself, and see how little we have learnt to make everyday outdoor activities bearable, let alone pleasurable. Yet we can do it even today. In the vast Park Hill housing development in Sheffield there are covered walkways (with shops) connected to the blocks of flats, and even on the exposed hillside where the scheme has been built one can move around in relative comfort. Without claiming that one could revolutionize society by sheltering many of our outdoor activities from wind and rain, it is conceivable that provisions of the sort I envisage could be a factor enabling people to spend more time out of their houses in company with friends and neighbours than at present. I am optimistic enough to believe that this would be a step towards greater feeling of community and home in its real sense.

So far, we have considered the creation of a home from the

planners' point of view. But the home in its fullest sense is equally dependent on the participation of the people who form the community, on their response and demands. At present we tend to do everything possible to frustrate the active participation of the community and are then shocked at the degree of apathy and the extent of social inadequacy and even delinquency which result from such frustration.

We do not even provide the most basic of community facilities in areas of new development or redevelopment. My survey of fourteen new towns built since 1946 shows that in every case social amenities have lagged way behind the provision of houses and factories. This is contrary to the spirit of the reports of the New Towns Commission of 1946 which led to the New Towns Act. These reports make frequent reference to the need for a full range of social amenities. They call for a balance of income groups and the need to avoid one-class neighbourhoods. They state specifically that segregation should be avoided. They suggest that multi-purpose meeting-places should be provided at the outset and that permanent buildings be provided *in advance of full demand*.[1] The failure of the new towns to carry out these recommendations is nothing short of scandalous.

So long as in any newly developed or redeveloped area houses and factories are built first and other social amenities follow on much later, if at all, the result will be an inward-looking, socially frustrated community, where every screw-head out of place in the house becomes a grievance and every blown fuse a disaster out of all proportion to its real importance. A encapsulated society, shut away in comfortable boxes in front of television sets, when it is not moving around in smaller boxes on wheels, must be avoided. Can we be surprised at the frustrations, disillusionment and boredom of a younger generation growing up in such an environment? No wonder they are all too ready to kick over the traces and tear away into one form of so-called delinquency or another.

Not only should we make the fullest possible provisions for people to develop a social life in new communities; we should find every possible opportunity to involve people in the planning and running of their own community. The great argument put forward

[1] New Towns Commission, Final Report, § B III, paras 25, 189, 190 (London: HMSO, July 1946).

1960s housing: Lillington Street, Pimlico, London (Darbourne & Dark, architects).
1950s housing: Churchill Gardens, Pimlico (Powell & Moya, architects).

1960s housing: Waterford Road/Fulham Road, London (Higgins, Ney & Partners, architects).

against any suggestion of this nature is always : how will it be organized and administered? We are so administration-conscious and so much in the hands of bureaucrats that any proposal which involves problems for an administrator is discouraged. When shall we get our priorities right? Do we exist as a society to make life easy for the bureaucrat or is he our servant?

At present the development of a new community involves two stages. At neither stage are the anticipated or actual inhabitants actively involved. Initially, in any new project, a community may not in fact exist. The future community exists only in terms of densities, family units or potential employees, commuters, never as people. Considerations of human requirements in anything but mathematical terms are excluded, since they might interfere with the correct computation of the planning formulae. Once a project is built and occupied the second phase starts. The administrators and housing managers take over and organize their commitments on an equally abstracted basis. People are hardly credited with human attributes : they become rent-books, problem families, digits. At neither stage are the future or actual inhabitants given a chance even to show or develop a real interest in their environment, let alone participate actively in its formation.

In the past the lack of human thought and imagination on the part of the planners and managers, in the social context, has been due as much to ignorance as stupidity. Today there can be no such excuse. Social surveys have shown clearly the human problems of communities and the inadequacies and frustrations which result from unimaginative development. Certainly it is possible to establish a whole range of information which is of vital use to the planner by surveys of existing communities and comparisons between them, in particular between old and new communities.

Under the present system demonstrable mistakes are made. Many of the errors and failures in the new towns could have been avoided if the planners had studied the reports made over many years on the development of Dagenham. This was, in its time, the largest housing estate in Europe and was started by the LCC in the 1920s as an attempt to solve part of the post-1914-18 war housing shortage. Today it would be called an overspill estate. Many of the recommendations of the New Towns Commission have their roots in

E

the failures of Dagenham.² Social studies and surveys are clearly valuable, but we must attach certain provisos. First, they cannot be treated as purely academic exercises by sociologists, to be filed away and forgotten : action must follow. Second, we must question the degree of inhumanity and paternalism which is attached to the scientific, objective and essentially uninvolved nature of the normal professional survey. The professional sociologists involved in these problems cannot be 'case-workers'. People are not 'cases'. The sociologists should and could be catalysts in the community, with the aim of enabling people to analyse their own problems and conditions and to think and act creatively about them. It would be even more valuable if the catalysts in the community were not just the sociologists but teams of all the professional people concerned in environmental planning. Each of them would have something to contribute through his own professional discipline. Perhaps even more important, each could learn a great deal about the community. In this way one would avoid the danger of the sociologist setting himself up as an exclusive expert on people.

The essential role of the professional team will always be to translate society's needs into appropriate building forms. In order to ensure that these needs are fully expressed, greater community participation is vital. Study groups could be formed, and these would be guided by the professionals. Schoolchildren have already taken part in surveys—on a national scale before the war in Dudley Stamp's great land-use survey, and more recently in many local 'projects' run by progressive secondary modern schools and by people like Richard Hauser and his Centre for Group Studies. The latter has developed a programme of social study and survey for secondary-school children which is being tried out in various parts of the country. One of the most important results in involving schoolchildren in social studies could be to break down the feeling of impotence in determining social problems. This is the root of apathy. If children can be encouraged to study, and even more important, to act, they may grow up less frustrated than their parents in this field. But this again requires considerable changes in attitudes on our part. We must also be prepared to participate in studies with our children and to act upon what we learn and demand what we

² See Willmott, *The Evolution of a Community* (quoted in Chap. 2 *n.* 5).

feel to be necessary. We must accept that young people could be one of the most vital creative forces in society, if we give them opportunity and responsibility and treat them as intelligent human beings rather than as animals to be tamed and broken in.

The fields of social study and survey must also be more clearly defined. In areas scheduled for redevelopment, studies should be made of existing communities. In new areas the future inhabitants should be selected and brought together as soon as possible and their needs and demands examined. There should be a programme by which groups of people in newly developed areas could be brought together at an early stage to help and advise newcomers. People should not be cast into a new environment without preparation. There should also be analyses on a continuous and comparative basis of newly developed areas, to determine degrees of success and failure. It is important that project survey, investigation of human needs, and assessment of success and failure in completed projects should take place on a continuous basis. It would seem natural that community groups be formed and instructed and helped in the techniques of carrying out such surveys themselves in a constructive and creative way. At the same time the human cost to society as a whole of social inadequacy, delinquency, crime, loneliness and even suicide makes it worth while to devote greater expenditure on such studies than at present.

A good deal of social survey work is being carried out. In particular, the work of the Research and Development Group at the Ministry of Housing should be mentioned, since this covers the field of pre-project survey of needs and requirements and post-project appraisal studies. Even so, there is an emphasis on user-requirements, statistics and technological innovation which may well mask the real problems. It is sometimes thought that such analyses will solve the problems of building for society. The argument is that if the physical properties of each type of building are studied and improved, we shall materially improve the physical environment as a whole. In fact all we may achieve is an improvement in the mechanics of building. And even if we advance much further than any present research and manage to improve the design of all our individual buildings, this will not necessarily create an ideal environment.

Apart from participation in the pre-project survey and continuing survey work, there are many other ways in which the community can and must participate in the building of its homes. Precedents exist for co-operative community projects both in Britain and the United States. In Britain we have, for instance, the co-ownership housing societies set up under the Housing Act of 1964 and under the general control of the Housing Corporation. In principle there is no reason why this system of participation should not apply to all State-subsidized housing. The job of the local authority would be to allocate a site to a number of families who would then form a management committee. This committee would appoint its professional consultants, in co-operation with the local authority and, with the consultants, plan and build houses and other community facilities, which would be administered on a non-profit basis. Anyone wishing to move would sell to the community for reallocation, and he could then buy in a new or other community with a vacancy. His rental payments would constitute a capital fund building up for him over a period of years, and this would enable him to have greater freedom of choice and mobility than most council tenants now enjoy. The key is co-ownership rather than the individual ownership proposed by the Conservative Party.

There have been many instances of local tenant groups being set up to counter some official authoritarian act. Unfortunately once the issue has been resolved there is usually nothing to sustain the life of the group, and consequently it dies a natural death or at most turns into a purely social club. In the few cases where such a group has turned its negative role into a positive self-determining one, its sense of purpose has acted as a strong influence on the local council's policy-making. It is this factor which is most significant : society has restored its basic democratic right, in that the permanent council officers are called on to serve and execute rather than dictate a policy. The real need is to ensure that from an early age society is made aware of its environment, its need to participate in its development and change.

The general adoption of a form of community-run housing and management could greatly ease the burden on understaffed local authorities. The trouble is that under the present system, where things are done by the State *for* and *to* people, when the sense of responsibility and participation is suppressed, society becomes apathetic and a greater load of responsibility devolves on the State. The situation gets steadily worse, with people less and less able to help themselves and more and more dependent on an increasingly bureaucratic authority. Political manipulation becomes increasingly possible for and even profitable to the powerful few. Inevitably, proposals for a radical change in the form and administration of building and social programmes will involve politics. But we cannot shirk them because we have always voted Labour or Conservative or are afraid of anything that hints even vaguely of something as un-British as communal organization, as a commune. We have a huge problem and unless it is tackled in a serious, radical way we may create a dead society for our children. Some far-reaching change in attitude is required and this may well result in radically different agencies for development from the ones we now have.

Chapter 8

The Professionals

In a world under growing pressure from increasing population, the physical demands of industrialization and urbanization, with all the problems of space, utilization of land and resources, pollution of the environment, the need for planning on a wide scale is now more or less taken for granted. The importance of professional specialists in the field of planning is also recognized. Yet the role of the specialist is often questioned by the so-called man in the street. In his often inarticulate comments about 'these bloody architects and planners' there is the same edge of fear combined with distrust that is characteristic of his attitude towards politicians. Probably the reasons are similar because the nature of their influence on him is similar : planners and architects as well as politicians are attempting to plan *his* life and surroundings in some measure and in a way over which he has limited control, whatever the political régime. It hardly needs saying that in present circumstances a rise in the material standard of living goes hand in hand with greater controls over the individual's physical environment and day-to-day activities. Whatever his degree of political freedom and social mobility, his actual sense of freedom seems to be more and more circumscribed. Indeed, it is arguable that his actual freedom is inevitably more restricted by a whole range of pressures at the same time as his opportunities, as a result of education and higher living standards, are apparently increased. Undoubtedly it is this sense of restriction of freedom and the frustrations that it produces which is largely responsible for the more extreme reactions of young people all over the world. It is by no means a superficial phenomenon. It is fundamental to the quality of human life.

The role of the planning professionals, amongst many other

specialists, is what particularly concerns us, in so far as it can be considered in isolation. In the first chapter I referred to the role of architects and engineers as professional men, and to the differences in their backgrounds and attitudes. Until its establishment as a profession in the nineteenth century the practice of architecture was based firmly on patronage, and its subsequent development has been essentially on the lines of patronage, formalized by a code of ethics in a way similar to the legal profession. It has developed in line with other professions during the nineteenth century and later. Initially, a formal method of training is established, with set examinations, usually after a group of practitioners has been set up to 'further the interests of the profession'. This is the first step in the process of restricting entry to the profession by enforcing minimum standards of attainment. As the profession grows in strength, with the recognition of its set standards as a sort of guarantee, it is enabled to remove competition in fee-charging and eventually to reach a closed-shop situation by some means of legal registration.

The profession of architecture has developed exactly along these lines. Today nobody can call himself an architect unless he is registered with the Architects' Registration Council of the United Kingdom, established by Act of Parliament. The condition for registration is that the architect shall have passed a qualifying examination, the only recognized ones being those set by the Royal Institute of British Architects which, though not the only organization of professional architects, has a monopoly in respect of such examinations. The result is that every intending architect must at some time belong to RIBA in order eventually to be registered with ARCUK.

I am not necessarily suggesting that there is something undesirable or sinister in this system. It does offer considerable safeguards and guarantees to the client. But, at the same time, it is important to be aware that the system has developed as a result of pressure from within the profession and not necessarily in response to a clear need of society. In claiming that this is the only possible form of professional service that is beneficial to society, contemporary proponents of the existing structure may be blind to certain real needs and problems.

The question requires scrutiny from two sides. First, what are the real qualifications that a professional architect involved in planning needs, and hence, how should he be educated and trained? Second, once qualified, how should he operate for the greatest benefit to society? Much time and research are being devoted to the training of architects and planners, but it often appears that the aims are obscured by technical paraphernalia. It is generally assumed that the practice of architecture involves a creative or artistic process. It is clear that this creative process has to be allied to a considerable technical knowledge in order to translate artistic concepts into practical forms. Administrative ability is required to supervise the whole process of designing, detailing and actually building. On this basis of design, technique and administration, most architectural education and training are constructed, with theory and practice involved at each stage. But what has as yet received scant attention in any depth is the whole question of social responsibility, both in direct terms of responsibility to a client who is often no longer a personal patron, but a committee, group or organization representing an anonymous section of society, and to the other members of that group or team which is involved in planning and building.

Architecture and engineering are not *per se* the only professions involved in building today: there are town planners, landscape architects, structural, mechanical and electrical engineers, quantity surveyors, land surveyors, interior designers and a number of other specialist consultants. If one includes the field of development planning and finance, there are in addition estate agents, building surveyors, valuers, accountants, lawyers and finance and investment specialists. If one takes the wider field of social planning, then the sociologist and other specialists in the field of social sciences are involved. In the field of building control and public health the medical profession is also concerned. And all this without mentioning the 'productive' side of the building industry, the builders, sub-contractors, manufacturers, suppliers and transport and plant organizations. In other words, the total scope of building involves an extremely wide group of specialists.

In the past the situation was simpler, just as the scope of building was simpler, the intervention of the State in the social services less, the scale of development smaller. On even a comparatively small housing project today, town planners will be implicated at the initial stages of planning control, an architect, quantity surveyor, land surveyor, structural engineer will almost always be on the scene, and often engineers concerned with the services will be involved either as independent consultants or in contracting organizations that will design and carry out the work. An estate agent's and lawyer's services will have been enlisted both at the stage of land acquisition and, in the case of a private development, for the final sale or lease. Local authority valuers will be at work, as will their engineers in building-control departments.

One of the greatest problems is that the co-ordination of all these people and their essential activities is by no means easy and can often be frustratingly difficult, since they are either each their own boss or at least not subject to the control of one interest. At the very best there is a three-way situation : the 'design team' of professionals employed by the client; the 'building team' of those who actually do the construction; and the 'control team' of public officials who regulate the buildings according to law and, ostensibly, in the interests of the public. The fact that there can be conflict between any two or even all three of these groups is problem enough; when there is conflict within a group the situation becomes virtually impossible, and it is sometimes a wonder that anything gets built at all.

What is evident first and foremost is that the training and education of all these people are almost totally unco-ordinated. Even the professions most closely linked in the building process, such as architecture, engineering, quantity surveying, have no common stage of training—unlike the various specialists in medicine, all of whom have the same general medical training before they begin to specialize. Perhaps this comparison is not altogether fair; but there is, from the social point of view, a common aim in both cases, the achievement of which depends in practice on teamwork and co-ordination. Yet, in the case of the building professionals, there is no formal acceptance of any need for common ground during a training period, which is often as long as a doctor's. True, architects learn the theory of structures, and quantity surveyors study building construction, but the importance of actually studying together and

F

appreciating the reasons why one man chooses to move in a particular field and the way he thinks, how he feels his work relates to the whole, is disregarded. It would seem to be self-evident that some degree of common training is essential if the design and building teams are to function effectively in the social interest, and in the interest of good building, which amounts to the same thing. It is precisely at this point that the professions and their organizations have totally failed to come to grips with reality.

As a result of their historical development, the professions have become responsible for setting the examinations and hence controlling the education necessary for qualifying in their particular field. They have all been concerned over the years in developing the standards and quality of the education within their control, and in particular in changing the form of education from that of the apprentice, or articled pupil, which was the most widespread form in the early part of this century, to full-time school or college education, which is now virtually universal. To that extent the opportunity exists for close co-ordination in education. Meanwhile, RIBA has pressed and is pressing for architectural education to be entirely within the universities. Engineering can be studied at university or polytechnics or colleges of advanced technology. Quantity surveying, however, does not exist as a university course. Building and estate management also only exist at polytechnic level. The one-sided demands of RIBA may well be understood by other professions as pressure for increased relative status in a situation where the latter have been catching up on the architect. Whether this is true or not, the fact that one profession is moving in a direction independently of the others, is not conducive to a long-term development of increased co-ordination.

In art education, which is very much in the throes of flux and change, the principle of a common 'foundation' year is accepted for all students before they go on to specialize. It is a pity that the foundation year is not always effective, but the principle seems to be sound. Yet there is far less need for professional teamwork amongst artists and certain designers than there is in the field of building. Interior design is dealt with at art colleges and follows the pattern of art education, which also seems strange in so far as the interior designer is very much a part of the building team. In fact

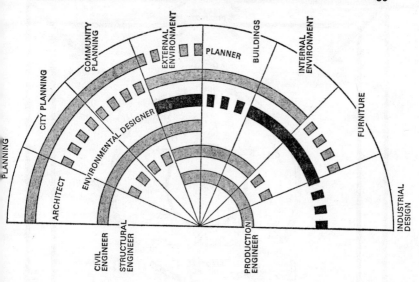

FIG. 17 Professional relationships: diagram prepared for students at Hornsey College of Art.

there are one or two Departments of Building Technology either recently established or in course of being established outside the university, usually as part of colleges of advanced technology. These will provide facilities for all the major fields of study within one institution, but the actual course structure will still not allow for a common period of training in general subjects for all students.

In the Interior Design Department at Hornsey College of Art which has designers and architects on its staff, there has been considerable discussion over the years on the subject of education and training of designers involved in the built environment, and a simple framework has been developed which sets out the subjects of interest to all the professions, and which develops those of special concern to the interior designer into a course structure. It also shows how the various specialists' work is linked and overlaps in practice.

The basic contents of common interest could easily form the framework of an introductory course for all students concerned with the built environment who would eventually follow the various

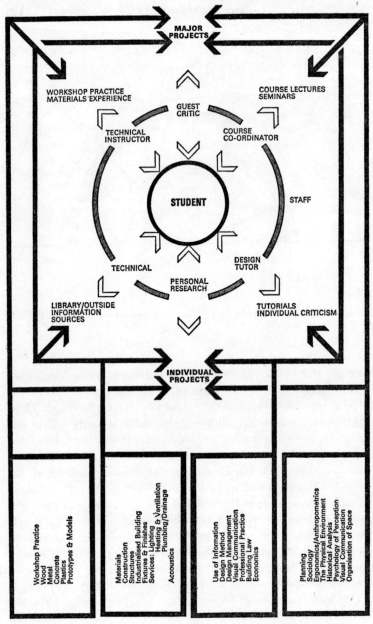

FIG. 18 Course structure for interior design students at Hornsey College of Art

specialist courses, and could be spread over a first year. The group work which is often used for studio projects in later years could be co-ordinated across different courses so that there was some experience at student level of co-operation with different specialists. The construction and administration of courses in the fields of environmental design should not present insuperable problems, and the outline I have given is but one of several possible forms they could take. The real problem is to get the professional and educational institutions to accept the need. This means their putting the general aims above sectarian desires. Someone has to take the lead, and in the present situation it may be that the only institution powerful enough to do so is the Government, through the ministries concerned with environmental policies and the Department of Education and Science. Since it is a subject of national concern, a clear directive from the Government would be appropriate.

Assuming that a more sensible form of training for professionals is attainable, how should they operate in society? I have mentioned the closed shop which already operates in most of the professions. In a situation where professional qualifications are necessary, if for no other reason than to ensure certain standards of technical competence, then it may be reasonable to require that anyone who wishes to practise should be qualified. Whether the individual professional institutions should continue to be the assessors of competence is another matter, particularly if we accept the value of co-ordination at all levels. It may be that a new body, representative of all aspects of the built environment, should co-ordinate the work of the individual organizations and become responsible for setting standards of competence and qualification.

The role of the professional institutions is not restricted to setting standards of entry: they are also keenly concerned to maintain professional codes of conduct which include the regulation of fees and aim to prevent a commercial form of competition between their members. This aspect of the architectural profession was called into question by the Prices and Incomes Board, set up by the Labour Government but summarily disbanded by the Tories in 1970, and is presently being discussed with RIBA. Yet the important issues seem to be missed whenever discussion is restricted to fees, and it is quite natural that the factor most closely affecting their income should cause the greatest concern to professional men. Nevertheless, the more important issue to them, and to the building industry as a whole, is the distribution and continuity of work.

If we can look at the professional side first, it is immediately clear that in Britain there is a relatively large proportion of architects in comparison with other countries. The profession of quantity surveying is peculiar to Britain, but is being recognized elsewhere as a valuable element in the cost planning and control of major projects. The availability of expert professional advice and service in building is considerable, and there are vast programmes of building, redevelopment and rehabilitation to be carried out. Yet the level of fully productive employment in the professions is never constant or evenly distributed, and is for the most part extremely erratic. It is very difficult for architects in private practice to plan their working schedules for more than about six months ahead, even when they have major projects on the drawing-board. They may be overstrained with the volume of work at one minute and have to cut back on staff and overheads through lack of work a few months later. Generally, this is not through any fault of their own, but usually due to changes in the national economic situation which affect investment by government or private institutions in the capital development which building represents. Then there is the problem of the small practices struggling to compete with the large ones, and the myth, currently propounded by their own professional institutions, that to succeed you have to be efficient, and that to be efficient you have to be big.

A large volume of work which is financed by public funds is dealt with by central and local government architects' departments. A number of official bodies, like the hospital boards and the nationalized service industries, have their own architects' departments. Many commercial and industrial companies have their own departments. Many building contractors are offering 'package deals' which include design done by their own architects. And all of these institutions also farm out work to private architects. The distribution of work is therefore rather complex and generally bears little relation to the average work-load of individuals. In no sector of architectural practice is there a guaranteed long-term programme, for even the government departments are subject to fluctuations as

a result of changes in the economic situation which affect government expenditure. In private practice it is every man for himself,
within the bounds of the code of professional conduct, and jobs are
obtained largely through personal contacts at early stages in a man's
career, and by recommendation later on, provided the architect has
been reasonably successful in securing work initially. This tends to
mean that younger architects are underemployed, regardless of
their ability. The successful architect is not necessarily the most
able; he is often the one who can compete most successfully in a
fairly tough commercial situation. Those who cannot compete may
end up working for a larger commercially successful firm, and may
well become partners after a period of years, or they may go into
public offices. But by the same token, many architects who work
in public offices and large private offices are either the less able from
a competitive viewpoint and in ability, or those who are seeking
security. There are a number who for social and political reasons
devote themselves to public service in public offices, but in my
opinion the ability and resourcefulness of architects in large public
and private offices are often of a lower calibre than is found in
smaller private practices.

In the situation I have described of uneven work distribution,
this means that much of the available talent is being wasted. If this
is true for architects, it is probably true for the other allied professions. In the building industry as a whole, one of the most serious
hindrances to the establishment of an efficient, technically well-
equipped and staffed industry is the risk involved in capital investment, and full-time employment for workers as a result of the
fluctuations in work volume. No other industry could exist effectively
with a labour force largely casually employed and as underfinanced
as the building industry. It is significant that the highest rate of
bankruptcy has always been in this industry.

If the distribution of work is as erratic and the flow of work as
uneven as I have described, how can effective teams of designers
be established who are able to carry out long-term programmes of
properly co-ordinated development? It seems to me that some
alternative to the present system needs to be found. RIBA has
carried out surveys of architectural practice and has established
many of the facts that lead to the conclusions I have summarized,

but apart from the comments on efficiency, which are not clearly borne out by the facts, and the pressure for larger organizations, which is only justified in terms of economic survival in the present highly competitive situation, no constructive suggestions have been made or, for that matter, are being considered, so far as I am aware.

If we look at the problem from the point of view of co-ordinating the work of the various professions, which seems to be essential if we are to achieve co-ordinated planning of the environment, then we must consider the possibilities of restructuring by developing teams, rather than groups or offices of single professions. When we do this it becomes apparent that there is a sort of numerical balance to be achieved as between one profession and another, since, for example, in terms of time spent on a specific project, the architect will probably take three times as long as the engineer or quantity surveyor. On this basis we can construct a diagram showing the sort of organization which will involve all the disciplines necessary, with a relative balance between the professions and their personnel (see Fig. 19).

Each group represents a building project; each triple group one environmental scheme; one complete group a major planning and development project. It would be possible to combine in a variety of ways to cover a wide range of projects, and have the full range of professional expertise at the disposal of the whole group. Essentially this is the way a number of the better large private and public offices operate today, but they probably represent a small minority of the whole of the allied professionals. What is desirable is that all those working in the field of environmental planning should both be working in teams and have the full range of expertise available.

Group practices have in fact been developed along these lines, but this has usually been done by a group of architects working in concert as opposed to a multi-professional team. As a step towards co-ordination, the professional organizations could set up a series of semi-public offices throughout the regional centres of the country. Consultants are often sought through the professional bodies by clients; if, instead of recommending an individual or several consultants for the client to select from, the professional bodies dealt with such requests by placing work direct with the appropriate

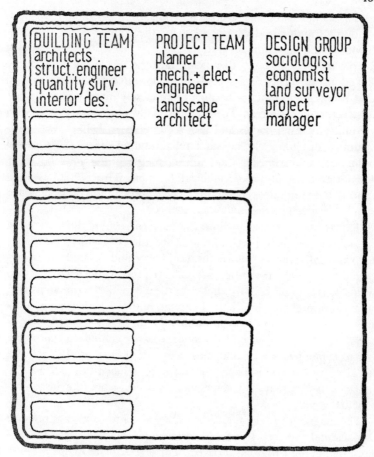

FIG. 19   The Design Team: possible organization for a comprehensive team of professionals

regional office, even those from government departments, then a fairer distribution could be achieved. This would benefit the younger or recently qualified professionals who could gain experience before going into private practice or joining more senior government and local authority offices. The professional bodies could appoint the senior members of the offices and ensure programmes of post-graduate training and development for the younger staff. Appointments could be made for limited periods in order to encourage people to move on into other fields, and the whole organization be linked to universities or schools of 'environmental technology' so that training and practice became more closely integrated and more of a continuous process. These offices could also work closely with voluntary housing bodies and local communities, helping with programmes of slum clearance and rehabilitation. The offices should be basically self-run, only accounting to the professional bodies if the latter have provided financial backing. This would avoid a central bureaucratic system; in fact the maximum independence should be given to the individual teams.

The relation of these teams to the local communities and the possibilities of their participating more directly with them could help towards breaking down the prejudices and misunderstandings of the layman about the professional. At present, the architect who wants to set up on his own, has to settle for minor conversions and small jobs, probably has limited capital, and works such long hours that he has no time for local affairs. At the point when he begins to meet with some success by way of a larger commission he again has to expand in a way that puts a premium on time. In any case his new assignment is likely to take him some distance from his office, a factor that will come more into evidence the larger his practice grows.

The magnet of London as a professional centre is always present. The capital city represents the desired place of business for the professional man who has 'arrived'. For one or more major projects the larger architectural practices usually set up regional offices. The projects more closely linked to the communities are handled by the overworked young architect struggling to keep head above water. If these jobs could be undertaken in circumstances offering greater security to the professional, and by a more effectively organized and backed group with permanent contacts in the community, the result would surely be an improvement in service on the one hand, and in relations and understanding on the other.

One should also consider how far the contracting industry could operate along similar lines. The biggest problem from the consumer's and the builder's point of view is in the range of small-scale building and maintenance. For years this end of the building industry has been the least efficient and most vulnerable economically. Nevertheless the scope is still vast, and in maintenance work growing. It is conceivable that the building trades, too, could be organized in the way suggested, and even linked to the consultants' groups for certain classes and scales of work. Once again, this would demand considerable rethinking in professional and business terms, but the difficulties are not insurmountable. Certainly they are worth tackling : reduction or at least stabilization of costs could follow and efficiency be increased.

Certain other advantages might accrue from the sort of organization on regional/local lines that I am proposing. Many of the problems that I outlined at the beginning of this chapter concerning the mistrust of professional planners involve those at relatively high levels in central and local government who, by virtue of their seniority, are remote from the people whose environment will be affected by their decisions. Years spent in the corridors of planning power cannot but erode to some extent the personal approach of all but the most power- and bureaucracy-proof individuals. Unfortunately, many if not most of these men have always worked in the high-powered situation, and the better their educational qualifications, the quicker they reach the heights. If, on the other hand, they were to spend a few years working in a local group before entering government service, they would at least be more aware of the 'grass roots' problems. Their previous contacts in such a group would allow for more direct, personal approaches and some red tape might be bypassed to advantage. Indeed, it should be possible to set up official lines of communication and to use the local groups to undertake studies and evaluate planning proposals made from above. The groups could provide the local 'expert opinion' in official planning inquiries and afford much help and advice which the local authorities' officers are not always able or in a position to give.

In the many cases where local authorities are too small to have their own well-qualified professional teams or where their remoteness makes it difficult to recruit well-qualified people, local groups could take on the work—assignments that in the present situation are often farmed out to private consultants anyway.

There is of course no doubt that this idea would be received with the utmost scepticism by contemporary professional bodies. It is hard enough to bring home to them the importance of co-ordinated teams. The proposal that they should join forces in organizing such teams as a 'third arm' between the private practices and public offices would be unlikely to generate any response, much less enthusiasm. Yet I am convinced that some radical change is needed urgently. I am also convinced that we must do more than pay lip-service to the idea of allowing people generally to participate in the important decision-making that will affect their environment. That the political system must find ways of enabling greater participation on the part of a society which is growing, or at any rate should be growing more aware of the problems, there is no doubt. That a closer contact between the executives who advise the politicians and carry out the planning, and the community at large, will help to improve the situation, is also certain. I think it highly likely also that many young professionals who dislike the idea of local and central government service, since they find the bureaucratic nature of such service creatively restricting, yet who feel deeply about social problems, may find a rewarding outlet in this 'third arm', instead of having to enlist in some large, commercially orientated private office.

Inevitably the process of co-ordinated training and working that I have outlined for the various professionals in the physical planning field will tend to efface the present rather rigid demarcations between one profession and another. However, I can see nothing but good in this eventuality. I think the effect will be for men to undertake and carry out work for which they are most suited, rather than because the name and status of their profession demand it. For too long the architect has claimed a monopoly of creativity and at the same time held on to certain aspects of project management and co-ordination for which he is not necessarily the man best qualified.

There has always been a fear, I suppose, that if you let control of a job out of your hands in any way then the end product will in some way suffer. In an age of individual commissions carried out by craftsmen builders this may have been true. In an age of large-scale building for relatively anonymous clients, of more complex and more industrialized building techniques, the management skills involved are of a different nature. The architect can easily spend much more of his time as an administrator than as a designer. One may well say that this argues for a greater degree of specialization in the professional field. Nevertheless, one of the better results of his traditional background is that the architect has always been and has certainly thought of himself as a man of wide interests, a sort of equivalent to the universal man of the Renaissance. This has produced arrogance on the one hand and a broad outlook on the other. We could well do without the arrogance, but it would be a pity to lose the broad outlook.

Closer co-operation among the necessary specialists and the consequent blurring of demarcation lines may not only help to preserve the broad outlook of the architect while sparing him some of the jobs for which he is not ideally suited, but may well encourage a broader outlook on the part of the other members of the team, who hitherto have had a more constricted range of vision. I can see no reason why there should not be creative engineers, creative quantity surveyors, and indeed it would be of great advantage to everyone if they all felt their jobs were creative rather than routine. Ultimately, in that golden age which even the most hard-bitten of us may sometimes dream of, one would hope that everyone would be creative and that the architect as a specialist would no longer exist; each man would build his own house. This does not seem a remote possibility in our present society, but there is no reason why we should not try to move a little way towards this visionary goal, particularly when circumstances are beginning to make such a movement not only desirable but at least conceivable.

Chapter 9

Education and the Environment

Throughout the discussion of the various aspects of environmental planning I have talked about assumptions that are made, sometimes false, sometimes true. It is clear that no particular group in society has a monopoly of either the true or the false assumptions. Certainly we have seen that the professionals have not necessarily made any fewer false assumptions than anyone else. The reason is obvious : in a field as wide and as socially important, the assumptions anyone makes will be largely affected by his general attitude towards society, the result of his upbringing, environment and education. Since the professionals are by definition middle class, whether in origin or through their individual mobility in the social sense, they will tend to have a middle-class view of society. At the same time, a vast amount of the work that they do involves planning and building for people of a different social class, with different backgrounds, education and outlook. To pretend that we have reached a classless society is in itself a false assumption, and we must therefore take due account of the problems inherent in the situation as it stands. To apply middle-class standards indiscriminately in the hope that everyone will either want them or will gradually achieve them anyhow, is to be extremely presumptuous, even arrogant. This problem largely explains or at least illustrates the gulf between those who are 'done to' and those who are 'doing', which I touched upon in the last chapter.

Accepting that there are differences, and that whatever social and political changes may develop in the near future there will continue to be differences for some time to come, how can the gulf be bridged? There is no doubt in my mind that it must be bridged if we are to provide a satisfying environment for everyone. In the last chapter I tried to show how, by a relatively small organizational change within the professions, the professional men working in the field of planning could get closer to the communities they were serving. Yet this would only be a small step, and would not necessarily produce much greater understanding of the problems of planning on the part of the 'general public' than it has of the medical problems of a group medical practice in the same community. In fact, people in general probably know more about health and medicine than they do about planning and architecture, partly because there has been a greater emphasis on health education and partly because of their personal contact with a doctor when they are ill.

In Britain there exist a number of societies that regard themselves either as watchdogs guarding against the incursions of insensitive planning or as crusaders trying to improve environmental standards. The first are those concerned with the preservation—now termed 'conservation'—of the countryside or of historic buildings and architecturally important areas of towns and cities. The second are organizations like the Civic Trust, which act more positively by encouraging improvement rather than by trying to stop desecration.

For all the good these well-meaning groups achieve, and their achievements are not inconsiderable, they remain firmly middle-class professional in outlook. For an architect working in London, their influence on the proposed redevelopment of an early Victorian terrace in, say, Camden Town, will be very different from that on a similar proposal in Holland Park. In fact, they would probably not even be heard in Camden Town. This is a sad but inescapable fact : the preservationists are very much concerned with retaining good middle-class residential neighbourhoods, whether they are urban, suburban or rural, and some of the specialist historical groups will fight for commercial and industrial buildings. But if a working-class area is scheduled for the bulldozer and is not part of a slum-clearance scheme, and this happens often, it will be up to the residents themselves to fight. Unfortunately the working-class resident is not usually a houseowner, and is rarely articulate or even self-confident enough to face up to bureaucracy on even terms. In the areas of acute housing shortage he is intimidated in all sorts of ways and it is this combination of factors which enabled the Rachmans to operate so disastrously in the overcrowded areas of many cities. It was for similar reasons that organizations like Shelter developed to help those people who were in need, were relatively poor, and inarticulate in a totally unjust situation.

As a practising architect I have myself been involved in a scheme in North London where an area of working-class housing surrounded by up and coming middle-class rehabilitated Victorian houses was being demolished by the GLC for redevelopment as local authority housing. Their proposed scheme was felt by local residents to be so insensitive to the character of the neighbourhood, the proposed blocks of four-, five- and six-storey flats and maisonettes being of so unimaginative and of so deficient a standard, that a local protest was organized. Utilizing the high proportion of architects and other professionals in the area, an alternative proposal was drawn up showing how a Victorian terrace of houses (which, incidentally, were selling for around £10,000) could be rehabilitated and new housing built on the remaining land no more than three storeys high, in character with the area and providing both more dwellings and a higher functional standard than the GLC scheme.

By their knowledge of the ways of approach to officialdom, local authorities and central government, this group was able eventually to get a scheme approved along the lines they suggested. But the original working-class inhabitants, mainly elderly retired railway workers, had been moved out with a considerable degree of in-dividual hardship, before the protesters had got under way. How many of them could move back if indeed they want to after a span of three years or so, is a problem. Certainly none of them wanted to move out. They had composed a small local community which had lived together for many years, and this was split up and dis-persed quite arbitrarily. They had not been consulted and it was only with the utmost difficulty that even the architects later involved in the protest were able to obtain details of the GLC's proposals for the site. This is certainly not planning for people; it is imposition on people, and in principle the only excuse, and the only reason the planners can get away with it, is that there is a housing shortage.

The essentially paternalistic nature of this attitude is no longer in keeping with the feelings and needs of society, if indeed it ever was. The problem is how to give people generally the knowledge and understanding to enable them to use the power which they could possess to achieve the rights which are their due. We are in fact arguing for real democracy in the field of planning the environment, and the key lies in knowledge and understanding. In principle this is one of the differences between the working-class and the middle-class man : the latter knows his rights, understands a situation and knows the best or most effective channels through which he can ensure that his rights are respected by the faceless bureaucracy which threatens him.

Yet, despite his ability to fight for himself, the middle-class man is still hampered by a considerable lack of knowledge and understanding of what is involved in planning and design. 'He knows what he likes', his tastes having been shaped by his background, and he knows how to preserve what he likes. But what he likes may be mock-Tudor, neo-Georgian or some other bastardized style. He may even have good taste in modern design, influenced by the glossy magazines and colour supplements. But essentially his understanding is superficial unless he has some special interest in the field. What is therefore clear is that there is a general ignorance about planning and design throughout society, and about the means of maintaining rights on the part of a section of society.

It is somehow strange that our educational system should fail so abysmally to provide instruction on the environment and the factors which affect it. After all, it caters to some extent for art and music, and certainly for literature. Perhaps this is really the nub of the problem, because for all the so-called art education in schools, the pattern of general education remains firmly rooted in literary subjects, and even in the field of science literacy in letters and numbers is the key to success. Visual perception counts for very little in our educational system. Yet our literary heritage developed basically from visual symbols. Children up to school age tend to draw naturally, and their drawings represent a means of expression related to their surroundings. As soon as they go to school, they are indoctrinated into the literary world : reading and writing have become so much the key to 'learning' that attempts are made to get children to read at even earlier ages than is now usual, and the success of such experiments are heralded as great steps forward in the educational rat-race. Drawing and painting are encouraged at school, and it is rightly stated that the creativity of children in many schools is being developed way beyond what was thought possible or even desirable one or two generations ago. Yet in terms of academic achievement, which is the criterion by which success or failure in education is judged, creativity means relatively little, and visual communication and understanding almost nil. Even the art-school courses are rated low-level unless they have a high 'academic content', enough to qualify for the Diploma in Art and Design. Visual perception and communication, not to speak of the visual arts, are therefore not taken very seriously, and only too often are treated as light relief in the otherwise hard grind of academic subjects.

There has been, and will certainly continue to be, argument amongst educators on the correct balance between science, the humanities and technical subjects. Somehow this has always seemed to me to be totally missing the point. It is very much like saying that town planning is the problem of land-use zoning. I hope that I have been able to demonstrate the falsity of that proposition. But in education we still classify by subject and areas of study, and those classifications more or less ignore the non-literary field of visual communication, and to a lesser extent of music, or treat them—since they cannot be wholly ignored in a 'cultured' society—with a certain degree of embarrassment. Even the range of literary subjects is treated with the minimum rather than the maximum of 'cross reference' and is rarely consciously related to the actual world we live in.

Essentially I would claim that we are only half-educating our children. By ignoring the whole realm of visual perception and communication, the history of the visual arts, architecture and the city, in relation to science, technology, social and political history, geography, biology and literature, we are perpetuating a society that is visually unaware and unobservant to the point of blindness.

This blindness is acute even among those who move on into the field of art and design. The number of students with whom I have worked in interior design courses who can draw little better than an eight-year-old, who look but do not *see* what the world is like around them, and who have to be retrained in the art of seeing and drawing during their first year, is so high as to present what strikes me as a very serious problem. I say 'retrained' because what we must do is to redevelop in the student the acute and enthusiastic observation and exploration of the visual world that are characteristic of small children, but that are almost totally destroyed in the educational mill. We will have to explain that the importance to the designer of drawing well is not that his drawings have particular importance in themselves, but that in learning how to draw one is subconsciously developing and sharpening powers of both observation and analysis.

If you sit down to make a ten-minute sketch of a building or a scene, using the simplest of media, you have first to select and analyse the essentials, those elements which are significant. You then have to convey them on paper. It is mental stimulus which helps to develop interpretive, communicative powers, and this should be a fundamental aspect of learning. The process of analysis and communication is the basis of design. Learning to see is the basis of understanding. Perhaps if the educators were able to understand this point they might begin to appreciate the importance of visual education as a parallel to literary education.

Unfortunately the camera and theories of modern art have both mitigated against the appreciation of these values, at least in so far as teaching is concerned. The various cults of abstraction and expressionism have been purveyed through art teachers to young people before they have been taught how to see and to communicate what they see. The child, learning to draw, normally goes through a period of simple, naïve drawing but consciously tries harder and harder to make his drawings correspond to reality. At the same time, his teachers will often self-consciously try to keep him at the 'naïve' stage or will encourage a conscious self-expressionist development, mainly because this corresponds more to their idea of contemporary art. In so doing, they will either tend to emasculate him or at least make him feel that what he is doing is not very important, but a sort of game. This is not mere conjecture: in interviewing students for art school I have frequently come upon statements which confirm this, and a general sense almost of guilt that they should be applying to a school to follow what they think may be a rather frivolous course of study. Anyone who at school expresses a clear determination to proceed seriously with his work in the visual arts, and does so, is regarded with misgivings. He is constantly under pressure to spend more time on academic subjects and to make sure he gets a good grounding in these, on the assumption that he must have 'his feet on the ground', since to be artistic is to be 'airy-fairy'.

The question of seeing and understanding, the uses of observation and methods of developing them, are used even today in certain educational fields. Just as the acting 'method', developed originally by Stanislavsky, depends upon acute observation and analysis of human behaviour, so similar ideas have been used particularly with backward children, to develop their interest and participation in the educational process. I have seen a demonstration by Richard Hauser with a group of secondary-school children, said by their headmaster to be hopelessly apathetic, which started with an analysis of how someone entered the room and ended with a lively and passionate discussion on the responsibilities of the group as a whole towards a wayward member of that group.

I have little doubt that the emphatically literary nature of our educational system leaves most of us with an enormous realm of untapped resources, and many of us at an acute disadvantage if we are not essentially literary people. There is a cogent argument for a reappraisal of the content of our general education on this very general basis. If we are concerned with the built environment and its design and quality, then there is an even more forceful reason to see that people generally are more observant and visually aware, and that they can understand both the background and reality of the present situation.

If we are to remedy the failings I have tried to outline, we must extend the scope of general education in three areas. First, in social awareness, social administration and human rights, both in the broadest terms, which would relate closely to social history, and to immediate problems. The latter could relate to local project work, which is carried out in a number of schools, and to local political and social problems. In fact, action groups of children could help in many local issues, both in research and activity. This possibility was mentioned in an earlier chapter and should be knit more consciously into the educational structure. Second, visual awareness, observation and communication should be developed considerably to begin to offset the imbalance which exists in favour of literary awareness. The intellectual potentials of this form of development need to be studied, and techniques worked out using the various media of visual communication to make possible a more effective and more serious overall approach. Third, the built environment needs to be developed as a 'subject' complementary to and relating with other academic subjects in a historical as well as modern context. The built environment, in this sense, should include the visual arts in their broadest sense, so that art is seen not as an unrelated luxury, but as an essential part of the human environment. Forget culture with a capital C, and think and teach about it as an inherent part of man's development.

These suggestions presuppose considerable rethinking about the educational process as a whole. I am neither competent nor presumptuous enough to begin to suggest what overall changes there should be. I do see that something is missing in the area in which I am particularly interested, and which affects the lives of everyone. This being so, I feel the educational structure must be changed in whatever way is necessary in order to accommodate what is lacking at present.

If these problems were tackled in the course of the general educational system there would be immense benefits to the professionals. I have earlier suggested that there is an urgent need for the professionals to start off on common ground. If their general educational background included what I have been suggesting, they would move on to their professional apprenticeship with comparable knowledge, a knowledge that would be shared not only by other professionals, but by everyone. Dialogue among different sectors of society would thus be eased and enriched by a common language.

The natural consequence would be a greater sense of participation in the planning processes by the community. Planners would have to account for their programmes, which is what many people rightly feel is not happening at present. Most important of all, it could lead to some control by people over their environment without so many legal restrictions; they might develop what is called taste and appreciation to an extent that would make it feasible for them to utilize prefabricated components in the way they wanted for themselves; do-it-yourself building at various levels might become a reality without chaos. This would make sense of the potentials in the field of industrialized building. We are really concerned with democracy, and we know that democracy only works politically with an educated and enlightened society. Such a society should reflect its enlightenment in its environment, and to do so requires enlightenment in that field as well.

Bibliography

The following is a short selection of books on some of the subjects discussed by the author, which may be of particular interest to the general reader:

Alderson, Stanley, *Britain in the Sixties: Housing*, Harmondsworth, Middx: Penguin Books, 1962.

Banham, Rayner, *Theory and Design in the First Machine Age*, London: Architectural Press, 1960.

Benevolo, Leonardo, *The Origins of Modern Town Planning*, London: Routledge & Kegan Paul, 1967.

Briggs, Asa, *Victorian Cities*, London: Odhams Press, 1963.

Buchanan, Colin, *Traffic in Towns*, London: HMSO, 1963; abridged ed. Penguin Books, 1964.

Carter, Edward, *The Future of London*, Harmondsworth, Middx: Penguin Books, 1962.

Centre for Urban Studies, London, *Aspects of Change*, London: MacGibbon & Kee, 1964.

Chermayeff, Serge, and Alexander, Christopher, *Community and Privacy*, New York: Doubleday, 1963.

Choay, Françoise, *L'Urbanisme Utopies et Réalités*, Paris: Editions du Seuil, 1965.

Coppock, J. T., and Prince, Hugh C. (eds), *Greater London,* London: Faber & Faber, 1964.

Corbusier, Le, *Towards a New Architecture*, London: John Rodker, 1927; Architectural Press, 1946.

Donnison, D. V., *The Government of Housing*, Harmondsworth, Middx: Penguin Books, 1967.

Doxiadis, C. A., *Between Dystopia and Utopia*, Hartford, Conn.: Trinity College Press, 1966.

Giedion, Siegfried, *Space Time and Architecture*, Cambridge, Mass.: Harvard University Press, 1954.

Gottmann, Jean, *Megalopolis*, Cambridge, Mass.: MIT Press, 1961.

Gruen, Victor, *The Heart of Our Cities*, London: Thames & Hudson, 1965.

Hall, Peter, *The World Cities*, London: Weidenfeld & Nicolson, World University Library, 1966.

Howard, Ebenezer, *Garden Cities of To-Morrow*, London: Faber & Faber, 1945.

Jacobs, Jane, *The Death and Life of Great American Cities*, New York: Random House, 1961.

Jordan, Robert Furneaux, *Victorian Architecture*, Harmondsworth, Middx: Penguin Books, 1966.

Lynch, Kevin, *The Image of the City*, Cambridge, Mass.: MIT Press, 1960.

Mumford, Lewis, *The City in History*, London: Secker & Warburg, 1961.
——, *The Highway and the City*, New York: Harcourt, Brace & World, 1964.

Osborn, F. J., and Whittock, Arnold, *The New Towns*, London: Leonard Hill Books (International Textbook Co. Ltd), 1964.

Pearce, I. H., and Crocker, Lucy H., *The Peckham Experiment*, London: Allen & Unwin, 1943.

Self, Peter, *Cities in Flood*, London: Faber & Faber, 1957.

Vernon, Raymond, *The Myth and Reality of Our Urban Problems*, Cambridge, Mass.: Harvard University Press, 1962.

Willmott, Peter, *The Evolution of a Community*, London: Routledge & Kegan Paul, 1963.

Index

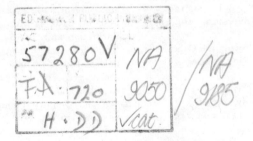